The
Best Ever Book of
Good
Clean
Jokes

The Best Ever Book of

Good Clean Jokes

Bob Phillips

BARNES
&NOBLE
BOOKS
NEW YORK

Published by Galahad Books
A division of BBS Publishing Corporation
450 Raritan Center Parkway
Edison, New Jersey 08837

By arrangement with Harvest House Publishers.

This edition distributed by Barnes & Noble Books.

Library of Congress Catalog Number: 97-77422

ISBN: 0-76074-586-2

Printed in the United States of America.

❧ A ❧

ABSURD

Jack: Aren't some of the clothes women wear absurd?
Frank: Yes, and yet they look so appropriate on some of them.

ACHES AND PAINS

Patient: Doctor, you've got to do something to help me. I snore so loudly that I keep waking myself up.
Doctor: In that case, sleep in another room.

∾

Looking down at the sick man, the doctor decided to tell him the truth. "I feel that I should tell you, you are a very sick man. I'm sure you would want to know the facts. I don't think you have much time left. Now, is there anyone you would like to see?"

Bending down toward his patient, the doctor heard him feebly answer, "Yes."

"Who is it?"

In a slightly stronger tone, the sufferer said, "Another doctor."

∾

Doctor: Do you remember what your husband's last words were?
Wife: Oh yes. He said, "I wonder how they can make a profit selling this red salmon at fifteen cents a can?"

∾

Patient: What can I do about my flat feet?
Doctor: Have you tried a foot pump?

∾

"I've been seeing spots in front of my eyes."
"Have you seen a doctor?"
"No, just spots."

∽

Have you heard about the amazing new discovery? It's a pill that is half aspirin and half glue for people who have splitting headaches.

∽

He is such a hypochondriac he won't even talk on the phone to anyone who has a cold.

∽

He's so full of penicillin that every time he sneezes he cures a dozen people.

∽

He always feels bad when he feels good for fear he'll feel worse when he feels better.

∽

Inscription on the tombstone of a hypochondriac: "Now will you believe I'm sick?"

∽

He's so anemic he has to get a transfusion in order to bleed.

∽

Ken: Have you ever had any hobbies?
Len: Let's see. I've had rheumatism and hives, and mumps—but I can't remember ever having hobbies.

ACTIVE

Visitor: Pastor, how many of your members are active?
Pastor: They all are! Some are active for the Lord and the rest are active for the devil!

ACTOR

And then there are people who claim movies would be better if they shot less films and more actors.

∽

A man walked into a theatrical agent's office, stood on a chair, flapped his arms, and flew twice around the room before landing on the agent's desk.

"How about that?" he said.

"Sorry," said the agent. "There's no demand for bird impressions these days."

ADAM AND EVE

Q: Who was the fastest runner in the world?
A: Adam, because he was first in the human race.

∽

Q: What did Adam and Eve do when they were expelled from Eden?
A: They raised Cain.

∽

Q: At what time of day was Adam born?
A: A little before Eve.

∽

Q: Why had Eve no fear of the measles?
A: Because she'd Adam.

∽

Q: Why was Adam's first day the longest?
A: Because it had no Eve.

∽

Q: Who introduced the first walking stick?
A: Eve—when she presented Adam with a little Cain.

∼

Q: Who was created first, Adam or Eve?
A: Eve. She was the first maid.

∼

The little rich girl came back from her first trip to Sunday school and told her mother, "Oh, Mummy! They read us the nicest story! All about a Mr. Adam and a Miss Eve and what a nice time they were having under an apple tree until a servant came along and disturbed them."

∼

Sam: My daddy has a sword of Washington and a hat of Lincoln.
Bill: My father has an Adam's apple.

∼

A Sunday school teacher asked Little Willie who the first man in the Bible was.
"Hoss," said Willie.
"Wrong," said the teacher. "It was Adam."
"Ah, shucks!" Willie replied. "I knew it was one of those Cartwrights."

∼

A Sunday school teacher asked her class to draw a picture illustrating a Bible story. One paper handed in contained a picture of a big car. An old man, with long whiskers flying in the breeze, was driving. A man and a woman were seated in the back of the car. Puzzled, the teacher asked little Johnny to explain his drawing. "Why, that is God. He is driving Adam and Eve out of the Garden of Eden."

∼

The little girl reported at home what she had learned at Sunday school concerning the creation of Adam and Eve: "The teacher told us how God made the first man and the first woman. He made the man first. But the man was very lonely with nobody to talk to him. So God put the man to sleep. And while the man was asleep, God took out his brains and made a woman of them."

༄

Q: When was radio first mentioned in the Bible?
A: When the Lord took a rib from Adam and made a loudspeaker.

༄

Adam and Eve were naming the animals of the earth when along came a rhinoceros.
Adam: What shall we call this one?
Eve: Let's call it a rhinoceros.
Adam: Why?
Eve: Well, it looks more like a rhinoceros than anything we've named yet.

༄

Adam was created first—to give him a chance to say something.

༄

Q: What is the first theatrical event the Bible mentions?
A: Eve's appearance for Adam's benefit.

ADVERTISING

It pays to advertise. Did you know that there are twenty-five mountains in Colorado higher than Pike's Peak which few people could name?

༄

Bill: Do you think your advertising has done any good?
Pete: Yes, indeed. Why only the other day I advertised for a night watchman and that very night my store was robbed.

African Chieftain

An African chieftain flew to the United States to visit the president. When he arrived at the airport a host of newsmen and television cameras met him. One of the reporters asked the chief if he had a comfortable flight.

The chief made a series of weird noises—"screech, scratch, honk, buzz, whistle, z-z-z-z-"—and then added in perfect English, "Yes, I had a very nice flight."

Another reporter asked, "Chief, do you plan to visit the Washington Monument while you're in the area?"

The chief made the same noises—"screech, scratch, honk, buzz, whistle, z-z-z-z-z . . . Yes, and I also plan to visit the White House and the Capitol Building."

"Where did you learn to speak such flawless English?" asked the next reporter. Again came the noises—"screech, scratch, honk, buzz, whistle, z-z-z-z-z," and the chief replied, "From the shortwave radio."

Age

Clara: My husband says I look younger in this hat.
Sara: Oh, really? What is your age?
Clara: Thirty.
Sara: No, I mean without the hat!

∽

You can tell how old you are if you remember when a family went for a Sunday drive and everyone got in the same car.

∽

The best way to cure your wife of nervousness is to tell her it is caused by advancing age.

∽

Several women appeared in court, each accusing the other of the trouble in the flat where they lived. The judge, with Solomon-like wisdom, called for orderly testimony. "I'll hear the oldest first," he decreed. The case closed for lack of evidence.

AGING

There are three ways to tell if you are getting old: first, a loss of memory; second . . .

AGREEMENT

You may easily play a joke on a man who likes to argue—agree with him.

AIR FORCE

A blowhard Air Force major was promoted to colonel and received a brand new office. His first morning behind the desk, an airman knocked on the door and asked to speak to him. The colonel, feeling the urge to impress the young airman, picked up his phone and said:

"Yes, General, thank you. Yes, I will pass that along to the President this afternoon. Yes, good-bye, Sir."

Then turning to the airman, he barked, "And what do you want?"

"Nothing important, Sir," said the airman. "I just came to install your telephone."

AIRLINES

Passenger: Say, Stewardess, this is the worst steak I ever had. Don't you stewardesses even know how to serve a steak? Bring me another steak right now!

Stewardess: Will that be to take out?

∽

A man is now able to go around the world in three hours . . . one hour for flying, and the other two to get to the airport.

∽

Stewardess: I'm sorry, Mr. Jones, but we left your wife behind in Chicago.

Man: Thank goodness! For a moment there I thought I was going deaf!

❧

An airliner flew into a violent thunderstorm and was soon swaying and bumping around the sky. One very nervous lady happened to be sitting next to a clergyman and turned to him for comfort. "Can you do something?" she demanded forcefully.

"I'm sorry, Ma'am," said the reverend gently. "I'm in sales, not management."

❧

Last week I was flying a plane and almost had a heart attack when I noticed a sign on the door of the pilot's cabin that said, "Student Pilot."

ALLOWANCE

Son to father: About my allowance, Pop. It's fallen below the national average for teenagers.

❧

Bob: I want to marry your daughter.
Dad: How much money do you make?
Bob: Two hundred dollars a month.
Dad: Well, her allowance is one hundred fifty dollars a month—and that'll make . . .
Bob: No, I've already figured that in.

THE AMERICAN WAY

Why do we spend five thousand dollars on a school bus to haul our children one mile, and then build a million-dollar gymnasium for them to get exercise?

ANCESTRY

The following conversation was overheard at a party attended by high society people:

"My ancestry goes all the way back to Alexander the Great," said one lady. She then turned to a second lady and said, "And how far does your family go back?"

"I don't know," was the reply. "All of our records were lost in the Flood."

ANGEL

A conscientious minister decided to get acquainted with a new family in his congregation and called on them one spring evening. After his knock on the door, a lilting voice from within called out, "Is that you, Angel?"

"No," replied the minister, "but I'm from the same department."

∽

A girl whose father was a photographer was out fishing with her parents one afternoon when a sudden storm came up and there was a brilliant flash. "Look," she said, "the angels are taking pictures of us!"

ANIMALS

Did you hear about the dating agency for chickens? It went bankrupt. They couldn't make hens meet.

∽

There were also the two very competitive silkworms who had a race. It ended in a tie.

∽

Q: What do you call a camel without a hump?
A: Humphrey.

∽

Q: What's worse than a giraffe with a sore throat?
A: A hippopotamus with chapped lips.

∽

Dopey: Why did the cow get a divorce?
Dopier: She got a bum steer.

∽

Woman: One of your bees just stung me. I want you to do something about it.
Beekeeper: Certainly, Madam. Just show me which bee it was and I'll have it punished.

∽

Q: How do you get dragon milk?
A: From a cow with short legs!

∽

"Did you know that it takes a dozen sheep to make a sweater?"
"Really? I really didn't know they could knit!"

∽

Two kangaroos were talking to each other and one said, "I hope it doesn't rain today. I just hate it when the children play inside."

ANSWER MAN

Q: What goes Ha, Ha, Ha, Ha, plop?
A: Someone who is laughing his head off.

∽

Q: What do they call cabs lined up at the Dallas airport?
A: The yellow rows of taxis.

Q: What do they call six women with one luncheon clerk?
A: Chaos.

Q: What was the largest island before Australia was discovered?
A: Australia.

Q: What do you call a crazy man who lives at the mouth of the Amazon?
A: A Brazil nut.

Q: What is worse than raining cats and dogs?
A: Hailing taxis and buses.

Q: What is the difference between a rooster, Uncle Sam, and an old maid?
A: The rooster says, "Cock-a-doodle-doo"; Uncle Sam says, "Yankee-doodle-do"; and an old maid says, "Any dude'll do."

Q: How many peas in a pint?
A: One.

Q: What kinds of animals can jump higher than the Statue of Liberty?
A: Any kind. The Statue of Liberty can't jump.

∾

Q: Who was King Midas?
A: He was the Greek king who fixed chariot mufflers.

∾

Q: Why did the priest giggle?
A: Mass hysteria.

ANTIDOTE

The medicine that kills dotes.

ANTS

Teacher: Why were you so late for school?
Student: I had to say good-bye to my pets.
Teacher: But you were two hours late.
Student: I have a large ant farm.

APOSTLE PAUL

Q: When was the apostle Paul a baker?
A: When he went to Philippi.

APPLAUSE

Applause before a speech begins is *faith.*
Applause during a speech is *hope.*
Applause when the speech is over is *charity.*

∾

Friend: You received a tremendous ovation. In fact, they are still clapping. What did you say?

Speaker: I told them I would not go on with my speech until they quieted down.

APPLE

While visiting a friend who was in the hospital, I noticed several pretty nurses, each of whom was wearing a pin designed to look like an apple. I asked one nurse what the pin signified.

"Nothing," she said with a smile. "It's just to keep the doctors away."

APRIL FOOL

Joe: When were you born?

Moe: April 2.

Joe: I see. One day too late!

ARMY

Voice: Hello. We need twelve vehicles in the parade square immediately. Two of them must be limousines.

Reply: What are the limousines for? To haul those fat-slob generals around in, I bet.

Voice: Soldier, do you know who this is speaking?

Reply: No, I don't.

Voice: This is General Wilson.

Reply: Do you know who this is speaking, sir?

Voice: No, I don't.

Reply: See ya 'round, fatso!

∽

One day a sergeant came into the barracks and asked his men if any of them knew shorthand. The recruits thought that it would be easy duty and raised their hands.

"Good," said the sergeant. "They're shorthanded in the mess hall!"

∽

Dad: When I was in the Army, Harvey, we had a drill sergeant who was so tough he used to wear a wig.
Son: What's so tough about that?
Dad: He used to keep it on with a nail.

∽

Reporter: And how did you win the Distinguished Service Cross?
Private: I saved the lives of my entire regiment.
Reporter: Wonderful! And how did you do that?
Private: I shot the cook.

∽

A soldier who lost his rifle was reprimanded by his captain and told he would have to pay for it.
"Sir," gulped the soldier, "suppose I lost a tank. Surely I would not have to pay for that!"
"Yes, you would, too," bellowed the captain, "even if it took the rest of your life."
"Well," said the soldier, "now I know why the captain goes down with his ship."

∽

"Look here, Private, this man beside you on this fatigue detail is doing twice the work you are."
"I know, Sarge. That's what I've been telling him for the last hour, but he won't slow down."

ATHEIST

Atheists are really on the spot: They have to sing "Hmmmmmm bless America."

∽

An atheist is a disbeliever who prefers to raise his children in a Christian community.

∽

Sign on the tomb of an atheist: "Here lies an atheist, all dressed up and no place to go."

～

They have all sorts of new services today. Now they've got a dial-a-prayer service for atheists. You call a number and nobody answers.

～

Pity the poor atheist who feels grateful but has no one to thank.

～

I once wanted to become an atheist but I gave up the idea. They have no holidays.

～

Three atheists were trying to bother a young Baptist minister.
"I think I will move to Nevada," said the first atheist, "only 25 percent of the people are Baptists."
"No, I think I would rather live in Colorado," said the second man, "only 10 percent of the people are Baptists."
"Better yet," said the third atheist, "is New Mexico . . . only 5 percent there are Baptists."
"I think the best place for you all is Hades," said the minister. "There are no Baptists there!"

～

An atheist was teasing Bill about his religious beliefs. "Come on now, Bill," he said, "do you really believe that when you die you'll go up to heaven and fly around with wings? I understand it's not warm up there like where I'm going when I die. How in the world are you going to get your coat on over those wings?"
Bill replied, "The same way you are going to get your trousers over your tail!"

～

Overheard: "I'm an atheist, thank God."

Atomizer

Now they've got a tranquilizer atomizer . . . one spray and it calms you down to the point where you can take a pill.

Attendance

"Does your husband attend church regularly?"
"Oh, yes. He hasn't missed an Easter Sunday since we were married."

Away from Home

"Those are fighting words where I come from!"
"Well, why don't you fight then?"
"'Cause I ain't where I come from."

B

BABY

Becky: Look at my new baby brother. The stork brought him.
Max: He looks more like a seagull dropped him.

❧

"What do you think of your new little brother, Dear?"
"I wish we'd thrown him away and kept the stork instead."

❧

On his first visit to the zoo, a little boy stared at the caged stork for a long while. Then he turned to his father and exclaimed, "Gee, Dad, he doesn't recognize me."

❧

Father pacing floor with a wailing baby in his arms as his wife lies snug in bed: "Nobody ever asks me how I manage to combine marriage and a career."

❧

An obviously pregnant woman was asked by another woman, "Are you going to have a baby?"
"Oh, no," replied the mother-to-be, "I'm just carrying this for a friend."

❧

Husband: Darling, I went in and paid the doctor with another fifty dollars today.
Wife: Isn't that wonderful! Just think, three more payments and the baby will be ours.

❧

Visitor: Does your baby brother talk yet?
Freddy: He doesn't have to. He gets everything he wants by yelling.

Bachelor

One who's footloose and fiancée free.

Bachelor Girl

A girl who is still looking for a bachelor.

Backsliding

A tramp knocked at a farmer's door and asked for some food.
"Are you a Christian?" asked the farmer.
"Of course," said the tramp. "Can't you tell? Just look at the knees of my pants. Don't they prove it?"
The farmer and his wife noticed the holes in the knees and promptly gave the man some food.
As the tramp turned to go the farmer asked, "By the way, what made those holes in the seat of your pants?"
"Backsliding," said the tramp.

Bad Driver

Despite what Ralph Nader says, the best safety device is a rearview mirror with a cop in it.

ॐ

A motorist is a person who, after seeing a wreck, drives carefully for several blocks.

ॐ

Nothing confuses a man more than driving behind a woman who does everything right!

❧

The motorist approached the coroner at 75-miles-per-hour.

BAD LANGUAGE

One day an elderly lady was shocked by the language used by two men repairing telephone wires near her home. She even wrote a letter to the company complaining about the manner. The foreman was ordered to report the happening to his superior. "Me and Joe Wilson were on this job," he reported. "I was up on the telephone pole and I accidentally let hot lead fall on Joe and it went down his neck. Then he called up to me, 'You really must be more careful, Harry.'"

BAD LUCK

Marty: Do you believe that you will get seven years of bad luck if you break a mirror?

Larry: Of course not. My uncle broke a mirror and he didn't have seven years of bad luck.

Marty: He didn't?

Larry: No, he was hit by a car that same day.

BALD

Bob was exceptionally bald. Bill was prematurely gray. One day these two met on the street and Bob said, "Bill, you are certainly getting gray."

"Yes," said Bill, "but I'd rather be gray than bald like you, especially since I learned the cause of both. Scientists claim that the roots of the hair grow in deeply and when they strike something gray the hair naturally turns the same color. If the roots strike nothing, the hair falls out.

"On the other hand," said Bob, "historians have learned that all barbarians have hair, which seems to prove that the less hair you have, the more civilized you are."

∽

It's not that he's baldheaded . . . he just has a tall face.

∽

There's one thing about baldness . . . it's neat.

∽

A bald man's retort: "In the beginning God created all men bald; later He became ashamed of some and covered them up with hair."

∽

Boy: Mama, why doesn't papa have any hair?
Mother: Because he thinks so much, dear.
Boy: Why do you have much, mama?
Mother: Because—oh, go do your homework.

∽

He's a man of polish . . . mostly around his head.

∽

There's one proverb that really depresses him: "Hair today, gone tomorrow."

∽

Today's toupees really fool people, but only those people who wear them.

∽

He has less hair to comb, but more face to wash.

∾

He's not baldheaded . . . he just has flesh-colored hair.

BAPTIST

Two men from the Far East were heard discussing the denominational difference between the Baptists, Methodists, and English Friends. One of them said to the other:

"They say these denominations have different beliefs. Just what is the difference between them?"

"Oh," said the other, "not much! Big washee, little washee, and no washee; that is all."

∾

Two ministers were discussing the question of how the Baptists originated.

First minister: That's easy. Anybody knows we Baptists got started with John the Baptist.

Second minister: You're wrong. The origin goes back a lot further than that. Don't you remember when Abraham and Lot were surveying the land of Canaan? They walked together for a long time, over the hills, across the streams, through the valleys. Then Abraham said to Lot, "All right, you go your way and I'll go mine." That's when the Baptist denomination got started.

BARBER

Did you hear about the rock and roll singer who wore a hearing aid for three years . . . then found out he only needed a haircut.

∾

A man entered a barber shop and said, "I am tired of looking like everyone else! I want a change! Part my hair from ear to ear!"

"Are you sure?"

"Yes!" said the man.

The barber did as he was told and a satisfied customer left the shop.

Three hours passed and the man reentered the shop. "Put it back the way it was," he said.

"What's the matter?" said the barber. "Are you tired of being a non-conformist already?"

"No," he replied, "I'm tired of people whispering in my nose!"

✂

A cute girl was giving a manicure to a man in the barber shop.

The man said, "How about a date later?"

She said, "I'm married."

"So call up your husband and tell him you're going to visit a girlfriend."

She said, "You tell him yourself—he's shaving you."

✂

"What happened to the other barber that used to be here?"

"Well, he is now in the home for the insane. One day, when his business was slow, he asked a customer if he wanted a shampoo and the customer said 'No.' I guess that was the last straw. He took a razor and slashed the customer's throat. By the way, how about a shampoo today?"

"Sure, go ahead," said the customer.

✂

Two barber shops were in red-hot competition. One put up a sign advertising haircuts for 75 cents. His competitor put up one that read, "We repair 75-cent haircuts."

✂

Customer (twice nicked by the barber's razor): Hey barber, gimme a glass of water.

Barber: What's wrong, sir? Hair in your mouth?
Customer: No, I want to see if my neck leaks.

∽

Barber: Haven't I shaved you before, sir?
Customer: No, I got this scar in the war.

BASEBALL

First Reporter: What shall I say about the peroxide blondes who made such a fuss at the ball game?
Second Reporter: Just say the bleachers went wild.

∽

Q: What makes a baseball stadium cool?
A: The fans.

BATH

"Did you take a bath today?"
"Why? Is one missing?"

BEANS

They serve a balanced diet in the Army. Every bean weighs the same.

∽

Husband: Beans again!
Wife: I don't understand it. You liked beans on Monday, Tuesday, and Wednesday and now all of a sudden you don't like beans.

BEGGING

Housewife: Why should a big, strong man like you be out begging?
Beggar: Well, lady, it's the only profession I know in which the gentleman can address a beautiful woman like you without an introduction.

Belch

"Sir, how dare you belch before my wife!"
"Sorry, ol' pal. I didn't know it was her turn!"

Bible Quiz

Q: Where is tennis mentioned in the Bible?
A: When Joseph served in Pharaoh's court.

∽

Q: What animal took the most baggage into the ark?
A: The elephant. He took his trunk, while the fox and the rooster only took a rooster and comb.

∽

Q: What man in the Bible had no parents?
A: Joshua, the son of Nun.

∽

Q: Who is the smallest man in the Bible?
A: Some people believe that it was Zacchaeus. Others believe it was Nehemiah (Ne-high-a-miah), or Bildad the Shuhite. But in reality it was Peter the disciple—he slept on his watch!

∽

Q: When was baseball mentioned in the Bible?
A: When Rebecca walked to the well with the pitcher.

∽

Q: Who is the first man mentioned in the Bible?
A: Chap 1.

∽

Q: When was money first mentioned in the Bible?
A: When the dove brought the green back to the ark.

～

Ned: What instructions did Noah give his sons about fishing off the ark?
Fred: I don't know.
Ned: Go easy on the bait, boys. I only have two worms.

～

Joe: Was there any money on Noah's ark?
Moe: Yes, the duck took a bill, the frog took a green back, and the skunk took a scent.

～

Q: Why didn't they play cards on Noah's ark?
A: Because Noah sat on the deck.

～

Q: How did Jonah feel when the great fish swallowed him?
A: Down in the mouth.

～

Q: When is high financing first mentioned in the Bible?
A: When Pharaoh's daughter took a little prophet (profit) from the bulrushes.

～

Q: When did Moses sleep with five people in one bed?
A: When he slept with his forefathers.

～

Teacher: Where was Solomon's temple?
Student: On the side of his head.

BIG JOHN

A very small, sickly looking man was hired as a bartender. The saloon owner gave him a word of warning: "Drop everything and run for your life if ever you hear that Big John is on his way to town."

The man worked several months without any problems. Then one day a cowhand rushed in shouting, "Big John is a-comin'," and knocked the small bartender on the floor in his hurry to get out. Before the bartender had a chance to recover, a giant of a man with a black bushy beard rode into the saloon, through the swing doors, on the back of a buffalo, and using a rattlesnake for a whip. The man tore the doors off their hinges, knocked over tables, and flung the snake into the corner. He then took his massive fist and split the bar in half as he asked for a drink. The bartender nervously pushed a bottle at the man. He bit off the top of the bottle with his teeth and downed the contents in one gulp, and turned to leave. Seeing that he wasn't hurting anyone, the bartender asked the man if he would like another drink.

"I ain't got no time," the man roared, "Big John is a-comin' to town."

BILLBOARD

Mark: Did you hear about the billboard on the side of the road? It was owned by an old man called Lang.

Clark: No, I didn't.

Mark: Everybody called it old Lang's sign.

BIRDS

There's a story going the rounds that involves a carpet layer who had worked all day installing wall-to-wall carpeting. When he noticed a lump under the carpet in the middle of the living room, he felt his shirt pocket for his cigarettes—they were gone. He was not about to take up the carpet, so he went outside for a two-by-four. Stamping down cigarettes with it would be easy. Once the lump was smoothed, the man gathered up his tools and carried them to the truck. Then two things happened simultaneously. He saw his cigarettes on the seat of the truck, and over his shoulder he heard the voice of the woman to whom the carpet belonged. "Have you seen anything of my parakeet?" she asked plaintively.

One time when my friend was in the breeding business, he crossed a parrot with a tiger. He doesn't know what it is, but when it talks everybody listens!

BITE

Joe: A panhandler came up to me and said he hadn't had a bite in two weeks.
Moe: Poor fellow. What did you do?
Joe: Bit him, of course!

BLAME

He wrecked his car, he lost his job, and yet throughout his life, he took his troubles like a man—he blamed them on his wife!

∾

To err is human; to blame it on the other guy is even more human.

BLINDNESS

During church services an attractive young widow leaned too far over the balcony and fell, but her dress caught on a chandelier and held her suspended in midair. The minister, of course, immediately noticed the woman's predicament and called out to his congregation: "The first person who looks up there is in danger of being punished with blindness."
One old fellow in the congregation whispered to the man next to him, "I think I'll risk one eye."

BLONDE

"What happened to that dopey blonde your husband used to run around with?"
"I dyed my hair!"

Boast

Bob was very tired of his friend Ken, who was always name-dropping.

"If you're such a big shot, why don't you go over to the phone, call the White House, and get the president on the line?"

"Okay," said Ken. He punched in a number and in a few seconds someone answered the phone. Ken handed the phone to Bob.

"Hello, this is the president," said the familiar voice on the other end.

Bob thought it was a trick. "Okay, that was impressive," said Bob. "But if you are really such a hotshot, why don't you call Buckingham Palace and let me talk with the queen?"

Ken went back to the phone and punched in a number and handed the receiver to Bob.

"Hello," came a distinctive voice. "This is the queen of England speaking."

Bob was very impressed, but still very suspicious. "All right, you happen to know the president and the queen. But if you're really a big deal, you'll get the pope on the phone."

"I'll do better than that," said Ken. Ken took Bob to the airport and they boarded a plane to the Vatican. There Ken disappeared, leaving Bob to mill about with the crowd in St. Peter's Square.

Suddenly the crowd became silent. Bob followed everyone's gaze to the balcony, where Ken and the pope stood side by side.

Before Bob could recover from his amazement, a man standing beside him poked him in the ribs.

In a heavily accented voice the man asked, "Who's that up there on the balcony with Ken?"

Boob Tube

A lot of old TV programs are going off the air and new ones are replacing them. But how can you tell?

❧

The longest word in the English language is the one that follows, "And now a word from our sponsor."

BOOKCASE

I now have 180 books but I have no bookcase—nobody will lend me a bookcase.

BORE

She: Whenever some bore at a party asks me what I do for a living, I say I'm a juggler with a circus.
He: And what do you do for a living?
She: I'm a juggler with a circus!

∽

"Well, I must be going."
"Don't let me keep you if you really must be going," said his bored host.
"Yes, I really must go. But, really, I did enjoy our little visit. Do you know, when I came in here I had a headache but now I have lost it entirely."
"Oh, it isn't lost," was the patient reply. "I've got it now."

∽

Young man: Yes, I know a great deal about baseball and football. I was also the captain of our basketball team. I drive race cars and motorcycles. I can swim and dance and I'm sure that you would have a great time going out on a date with me. I am a good conversationalist.
Young lady: Do you have a group photograph of yourself?

BORED

After a long, dry sermon, the minister answered that he wished to meet with the church board following the close of the service. The first man to arrive was a stranger.
"You misunderstood my announcement. This is a meeting of the board," said the minister.
"I know," said the man, "but if there is anyone here more bored than I am, I'd like to meet him."

BOUQUETS

First Actor: What's the matter with the leading lady?
Second Actor: She only got nine bouquets of flowers tonight.
First Actor: Good heavens! Isn't that enough?
Second Actor: Nope, she paid for ten.

BOXING

Boxing coach: You did a terrible job out there. If I were as big as you,
I would be heavyweight champion of the world.
Boxer: Why don't you become the lightweight champion?

BOY MEETS FATHER

Father: Sue, what are you doing out there?
Sue: I'm looking at the moon.
Father: Well, tell the moon to go home. It's half-past eleven.

∽

Boy: I'd like to marry your daughter.
Father: Have you seen my wife yet?
Boy: I have . . . but I prefer your daughter.

BOY MEETS GIRL

"Why does my sweetheart always close her eyes when I kiss her?"
"Look in the mirror and you'll know."

∽

John: You must marry me . . . I love you, there can be no other . . .
Mary: But, John, I don't love you . . . you must find some other woman
. . . some beautiful woman . . .
John: But I don't want a beautiful woman . . . I want you.

∽

Boy: You know, sweetheart, since I met you, I can't eat . . . I can't sleep . . . I can't drink.
Girl: Why not?
Boy: I'm broke.

∽

"My girlfriend takes advantage of me."
"What do you mean?"
"I invited her out to dinner and she asked me if she could bring a date!"

∽

After a blind date a fellow said to his friend, "After I got home last night, I felt a lump in my throat."
"You really like her, huh?"
"No, she's a karate expert."

∽

"Do you have the book *Man, Master of Women?*" a young man asked the lady librarian.
"Fiction counter to your left," the librarian replied.

∽

Boy (with one hand cupped over the other): If you can guess what I have in my hand, I'll take you out tonight.
Girl: An elephant!
Boy: Nope! But that's close enough. I'll pick you up at 7:30.

∽

Boy: Ah, look at the cow and the calf rubbing noses in the pasture. That sight makes me want to do the same.
Girl: Well, go ahead . . . it's your cow.

∽

Girl: Do you think you could be happy with a girl like me?
Boy: Perhaps, if she isn't too much like you.

∽

"How come you go steady with Eloise?"
"She's different from other girls."
"How so?"
"She's the only girl who will go with me."

❧

He: Oh, my dear, how can I leave you?
She: By train, plane, or taxi!

❧

Boy: Gladys, do you love me?
Girl: Yeah.
Boy: Would you be willing to live on my income?
Girl: Yes, if you'll get another for yourself.

❧

Boy: Darling, I've lost all my money. I haven't got a cent in the world.
Girl: That won't make any difference, dear. I'll love you just as much—even if I never see you again.

❧

Bill: That girl in the red dress isn't very smart.
Phil: I know. She hasn't paid any attention to me, either.

❧

Harry: My girlfriend has a huge lower lip, but I don't mind.
Gary: You don't?
Harry: No, her upper lip covers it!

❧

She: Look at my engagement ring!
Chi-Chi: That's a lovely ring. It's nice to know you're not marrying a spendthrift.

❧

Boy: Boy, if I had a nickel for every girl I'd kissed . . .
Girl: You'd be able to buy a pack of gum!

BOYFRIEND AND GIRLFRIEND

"When I went out with Fred, I had to slap his face five times."
"Was he that fresh?"
"No! I thought he was dead!"

ↀ

Harry: Please give me a kiss.
Carrie: My lips are chapped.
Harry: Well, one more chap won't hurt them.

ↀ

"Well, and how are you getting on with your courtship of the banker's daughter?"
"Not so bad. I'm getting some encouragement now."
"Really, is she beginning to smile sweetly on you or something?"
"Not exactly, but last night she told me she had said 'no' for the last time."

ↀ

Rod: I'm through with that girl.
Doug: Oh, why?
Rod: She asked me if I danced.
Doug: Well, what's wrong with that?
Rod: I was dancing with her when she asked me.

ↀ

Winking at a girl in the dark is like doing business without advertising: You know what you are doing, but nobody else does.

ↀ

Girl: I'm telling you for the last time; you can't kiss me!
Boy: Oh, I knew you would weaken.

ↀ

John: Don't you think I'm rather good looking?
Judy: In a way.
John: What kind of way?
Judy: A way off.

∽

Girl: Did you kiss me when the lights were out?
Boy: No!
Girl: It must have been that fellow over there!
Boy (starting to get up): I'll teach him a thing or two!
Girl: You couldn't teach him a thing!

∽

John: I can't seem to get anywhere with Jan.
Jack: What happened?
John: I told her I was knee-deep in love with her.
Jack: What was her reaction?
John: She promised to put me on her wading list.

∽

Father: Did Paul bring you home last night?
Daughter: Yes, it was late, Daddy. Did the noise disturb you?
Father: No, my dear, it wasn't the noise. It was the silence.

∽

First boy: She has a beautiful pair of eyes, her skin has the glow of a peach, her cheeks are like apples, and her lips like cherries—that's my girl.
Second boy: Sounds like a fruit salad to me.

BRAINS

Look, I'm not going to engage in a battle of wits with you. I never attack anyone who's unarmed.

∽

"It took me all morning to fill this salt shaker."
"Why all morning?"
"It's *hard* to get the salt through those little holes on the top!"

∾

The reason ideas die quickly in some people's heads is because they can't stand solitary confinement.

∾

Husband: I hear that fish is brain food.
Wife: You had better eat a whale.

∾

He had an extremely high IQ when he was five. Too bad he grew out of it.

∾

I wish I had a lower IQ so I could enjoy your company.

∾

You know, if brains were dynamite, he wouldn't have enough to blow his nose!

∾

Harry: I'm putting everything I know into my next story.
Carry: I get it—a short story.

∾

You must be a twin . . . no one person could be that stupid.

∾

You can fool some of the people all of the time and all of the people some of the time, but most of the time they will make fools of themselves.

༖

"You're not smart enough to talk to an idiot!"
"Okay! I'll send you a letter!"

Bridal

A harness for a man.

Brush Your Teeth

Teacher: Why don't you brush your teeth? I can see what you had for breakfast this morning.
Student: What did I have?
Teacher: Eggs!
Student: You're wrong! That was yesterday!

Bums

Two bums were discussing the reasons they became bums.
"I'm the fellow who never listened to anybody," said the first bum.
"Shake, partner," said the second bum. "I'm the man who followed everybody's advice."

Burglars

The burglars had tied and gagged the bank cashier after extracting the combination to the safe and had herded the other employees into a separate room under guard. After they rifled the safe and were about to leave, the cashier made desperate pleading noises through the gag. Moved by curiosity, one of the burglars loosened the gag.

"Please," whispered the cashier, "take the books, too. I'm $8,500 short."

❧

Jan: Wake up, John. There's a burglar going through your pants pockets.

John: Oh, you two just fight it out between yourselves.

❧

A burglar, needing money to pay his income taxes, decided to burgle the safe in a store. On the safe door he was very pleased to find a note reading: "Please don't use dynamite. The safe is not locked. Just turn the knob." He did so. Instantly a heavy sandbag fell on him, the entire premises were floodlighted, and alarms started clanging. As the police carried him out on a stretcher, he was heard moaning: "My confidence in human nature has been rudely shaken."

❧

Husband: Yesterday, a burglar got in the house.

Friend: Did he get anything?

Husband: I'll say. My wife thought I was coming home late.

❧

Jess: Did you hear about the fellow who stole the calendar?

Ray: No, what happened?

Jess: He got twelve months.

BUSINESS

A young man came to interview a bank president.

"Tell me, Sir, how did you become so successful?"

"Two words."

"And what are they, Sir?"

"Right decisions."

"How do you make right decisions?"
"One word . . . experience."
"And how do you get experience?"
"Two words."
"And what are they?"
"Wrong decisions!"

∽

March is a very dangerous month in which to speculate in stocks. The other months are April, May, June, July, August, September, October, November, December, January, and February.

∽

Get my broker, Miss Smith.
Yes, sir—stock or pawn?

∽

Advertising manager: Where did you get this wonderful follow-up system? It would drag money out of anybody.
Assistant: I'll say it would. It's compiled from the letters my son wrote me from college.

∽

The head of a small industrial concern posted DO IT NOW signs all around his office and plant in the hope of getting better results from his workers. Some weeks later, when asked why he was removing the slogans, he said: "It worked too well: the bookkeeper skipped with $20,000; the chief copy eloped with the best secretary I've ever had; three salesmen asked for raises; the workers in the factory joined the union and are out on strike; and the office boy threatened to beat me up."

∽

An executive is a person who can take two hours for lunch without anyone missing him.

BUTCHER

Customer: What is the price of hamburger?

Butcher: One dollar and forty cents a pound.

Customer: One dollar and forty cents! The store down the street sells it for one dollar and fifteen cents a pound.

Butcher: Why don't you go there to shop?

Customer: I did, but they are all out of hamburger.

Butcher: Well, when I am out of hamburger, I sell it for a dollar a pound.

∽

Woman: I want a piece of beef, and make it lean.

Butcher: Certainly, madam. Which way?

CALVIN COOLIDGE

When someone complained to Calvin Coolidge about his habitual silence he replied, "Well, I found out early in life that you didn't have to explain something you hadn't said."

CAMP

Summertime is when parents pack off their troubles to an old Indian Camp and smile, smile, smile!

～

Did you hear about the parents who sent their young son to camp to learn how to make decisions of his own? He did—the second day there he decided to come home.

CANNIBALS

It was a lucky day in the cannibal village. They had an explorer in the pot, and about to be cooked. The chief asked the victim if he had any last words to say. The explorer gasped, "Yes. I'm smoking more now and enjoying it less."

～

My uncle is a cannibal. He's been living on us for twenty years!

～

Cannibal Cook: Shall I stew both of these Navy cooks?
Cannibal King: No. One's enough. Too many cooks spoil the broth.

～

Joe: What would a cannibal be if he ate his mother's sister?
Moe: I give up.
Joe: An aunteater.

⤸

First Cannibal: We've just captured a movie star.
Second Cannibal: Great! I was hoping for a good ham sandwich.

⤸

Most cannibal jokes aren't in good taste.

Cars

Unable to find a replacement cog for his car engine, a Datsun owner was told that he would have to go to Japan to get one.

He didn't want to make the trip for so little, so he decided to buy six-dozen cogs and bring them back to America and sell them, to help pay for the flight.

On the flight back, there was engine trouble and to save fuel the pilot gave orders to jettison all baggage. This meant that the cogs had to go also.

On the ground below, an elderly couple looked up at the sky. They saw all the baggage falling from the plane.

"Look, Sarah," said the old man. "It's raining Datsun cogs."

⤸

Gas prices are so high that when I pulled into a station this morning and asked for a dollar's worth, the attendant dabbed some behind my ears.

⤸

Did you hear about the man who bought one of those British cars? He kept careful records for a month because everybody said the mileage was so sensational. Obviously, he wasn't getting what he was supposed to be getting. So he took the car to the mechanic and told him to check it out. The car was in perfect condition. The owner protested, "Look, I love this car, but evidently I am not getting the mileage that I am supposed to be getting." The mechanic looked at him and said, "Why don't you do what all other foreign car owners do?" "What's that?" "Lie about it."

Car Sickness

The feeling you get every month when the payment is due.

Carp

Did you hear about the fellow who went carp fishing? As he was about to throw his first cast, his wallet fell out of his pocket into the lake. A carp grabbed the wallet and started to swim away with it. Suddenly, another carp ate the carp that had eaten the wallet. Then, yet another, even larger carp came along and swallowed the carp that ate the carp that devoured the wallet.

And that's how carp-to-carp walleting began.

Catskill

Heckle: Did you ever see the Catskill mountains?
Jeckle: No, but I've seen what cats do to mice.

Chandelier

During a business meeting in a small mountain church, one of the deacons said, "Pastor, I think we need a chandelier for the church."

"No," replied another deacon. "I'm against it."

"Why don't you think we need a chandelier, brother deacon?" asked the pastor.

"Well, first, nobody in the church can spell it; second, nobody in the church can play it; and, third, what this church needs, above all else, is mo' light!"

Change the Rope

An old European monastery is perched high on a 500-foot cliff. Visitors ride up in a big basket, pulled to the top with a ragged old rope.

Halfway up, a passenger nervously asked: "How often do you change the rope?"

The monk in charge replied: "Whenever the old one breaks."

Chauvinism

HOW TO TELL A BUSINESSMAN FROM A BUSINESS-WOMAN:

A businessman is dynamic; a businesswoman is aggressive.

He is good on details; she is picky.

He loses his temper; she is crabby.

He's a go-getter; she is pushy.

When he's depressed, everyone tiptoes past his office; when she is moody, it must be her time of the month.

He follows through; she doesn't know when to quit.

He's confident; she is stuck-up.

He stands firm; she's hard as nails.

He has the courage of his convictions; she is stubborn.

He is a man of the world; she's been around.

He can handle his liquor; she's a lush.

He isn't afraid to say what he thinks; she's mouthy.

He's human; she's emotional.

He exercises authority diligently; she is power-mad.

He is closemouthed; she is secretive.

He can make quick decisions; she's impulsive.

He runs a tight ship; she's hard to work for.

Chicken Chow Mein

"I was a kamikaze flier during the war," said a Japanese man who was named Chow Mein.

"How could that be? That was a suicide squad."

"Oh, they called me Chicken Chow Mein."

CHILDREN

Little Susan was Mother's helper. She helped set the table when company was due for dinner. Presently everything was on, the guest came in, and everyone sat down. Then Mother noticed something missing. "Susan," she said, "You didn't put a knife and fork at Mr. Larson's place."

"I thought he wouldn't need them," explained Susan. "Daddy said he always eats like a horse."

∽

Mother: Eat your spinach. Think of the thousands of starving children who would love some spinach like this.

Billy: Name two.

∽

Mother: Suzie, what have you been doing this morning while I was working in the kitchen?

Suzie: I was playing postman.

Mother: How could you play postman when you don't have any letters?

Suzie: I was looking through your trunk in the garage and found a packet of letters tied with a nice ribbon, and I posted one in everyone's mailbox on the block.

CHINA

"What do you think of Red China?" one lady asked another during a luncheon on world affairs.

"Oh, I don't know," replied the other lady. "I guess it would be all right if you used it on a yellow tablecloth."

CHRISTMAS

There's nothing like the Christmas season to put a little bounce in your checks.

∽

A little boy excited about his part in the Christmas play came home and said:

"I got a part in the Christmas play!"

"What part?" asked his mother.

"I'm one of the three wise guys!" was the reply.

CHURCH

A man had been shopping around for a church home when he stopped in one church just in time to hear the pastor say, "We have left undone those things which we ought to have done these things which we ought not to have done."

The man dropped into a pew and sighed with relief, "I've found my crowd at last."

∾

A businessman happened to be staying in a hotel where a group of ministers was holding a conference. The next morning was very cold and as the businessman approached the dining room, he noticed the ministers gathered around a blazing log fire in the dining area. He was freezing and tried to get close to the fire but the ministers blocked the way. The businessman sat for a few minutes shivering in the cold. Suddenly he shouted, "Last night I dreamed I was in hell."

"Really?" said one of the ministers. "What was it like?"

The businessman replied, "Not much different than right here. I couldn't get near the fire, for all the ministers were in the way."

∾

I spoke in one church that was so small that when I took a bow I hit my head on the back pew.

∾

The chief trouble with the church is that you and I are in it.

∾

Wife: Did you see that hat Mrs. Jones wore to church?
Husband: No.
Wife: Did you see the new dress Mrs. Smith had on?
Husband: No!
Wife: A lot of good it does you to go to church!

∽

You can always tell a church that isn't doing well. The Cadillac they raffle off is used.

∽

A church is an organization supported by the husbands of its members.

∽

Some go to church to take a walk;
Some go there to laugh and talk;
Some go there to meet a friend;
Some go there their time to spend;
Some go there to meet a lover;
Some go there a fault to cover;
Some go there for speculation;
Some go there for observation;
Some go there to doze and nod;
The wise go there to worship.

∽

An usher went up to a man with his hat on in church and asked him to remove it. "Thank goodness," said the man. "I thought that would do it. I've attended this church for months, and you are the first person who has spoken to me."

∽

Jack: Do you know Pete Wilson?
Mack: I sure do. We slept in the same church pew for over fifteen years.

∽

"I never go to church," boasted a wandering member. "Perhaps you have noticed that?"

"Yes, I have noticed that," said his pastor.

"Well, the reason I don't go is that there are so many hypocrites there."

"Oh, don't let that keep you away," replied the pastor, smiling blandly. "There is always room for one more, you know."

❧

Right in the middle of the service and just before the sermon, a member of the congregation remembered she had forgotten to turn off the gas under the roast. Hurriedly she scribbled a note and passed it to the usher to give to her husband. Unfortunately, the usher misunderstood her intention and took it to the pulpit. Unfolding the note, the preacher read aloud, "Please go home and turn off the gas."

❧

A man was going to attend a Halloween party dressed in a costume of the devil. On his way it began to rain, so he darted into a church where a revival meeting was in progress.

At the sight of his devil's costume, people began to scatter through the doors and windows.

One lady got her coat sleeve caught on the arm of one of the seats and, as the man came closer, she pleaded, "Satan, I've been a member of this church for twenty years, but I've really been on your side all the time."

❧

Some go to church to weep, while others go to sleep.
Some go to tell their woes, others to show their clothes.
Some go to hear the preacher, others like the solo screecher.
Boys go to reconnoiter, girls go because they orter.
Many go for good reflections, precious few to help collections.

CHURCH ATTENDERS

Every church has, in addition to the brakeman, a construction and a wrecking crew. To which do you belong? One of them for sure.

❧

Every church has three classes of members: the workers, the jerkers, and the shirkers.

∽

There are four classes of church members: the tired, the retired, the tiresome, and the tireless.

∽

It seems that some church members have been starched and ironed, but too few have been washed.

Church Bulletin Boards

No matter how much you nurse a grudge, it won't get better.

∽

Start living to beat hell.

∽

If some people lived up to their ideals, they would be stooping.

∽

Everything you always wanted to know about heaven and hell but were afraid to ask.

∽

Pray up in advance.

∽

Patience is the ability to stand something as long as it happens to the other fellow.

∽

Visitor: Pastor, how many active members do you have?

Minister: They're all active. Half of them are working with me and half are working against me.

CIGARS

A defendant in a lawsuit involving a large sum of money was talking to his lawyer.

"If I lose the case, I'll be ruined," he said.

"It's in the judge's hands now," said the lawyer.

"Would it help if I sent the judge a box of cigars?"

"Oh, no," said the lawyer. "This judge is a stickler for ethical behavior. A stunt like that would prejudice him against you. He might even hold you in contempt of court. In fact, you shouldn't even smile at the judge."

Within the course of time, the judge rendered a decision in favor of the defendant.

As the defendant left the courthouse with his lawyer, he said, "Thanks for the tip about the cigars. It worked."

"I'm sure we would have lost the case if you had sent them."

"But I did send them."

"You did?"

"Yes. That is how we won the case."

"I don't understand," said the lawyer.

"It's easy. I sent the cigars to the judge, but enclosed my opponent's business card."

CLEAVER

Did you hear about the inventor who came up with a knife that would slice two loaves of bread at the same time? He sold it to a large bakery. He then developed a knife that could slice three loaves of bread at the same time. He sold that idea, too.

Finally, the ultimate. He made a huge knife that could cut four loaves of bread at the same time! And so was born the world's first four-leaf cleaver.

CLERGY

Two men named Richard Hanson lived near each other in the same community. One was a minister and the other was a businessman. The minister passed away at about the same time as the businessman went on a trip to Florida.

When the businessman arrived in Florida he sent a telegram to his wife informing her of his safe arrival. Unfortunately, the message was delivered in error to the wife of the recently deceased minister.

The telegraph read, "ARRIVED SAFELY; HEAT HERE TERRIFIC."

∽

(The following is a story that can be told about a clergyman or friend.)

One day I had a dream about my friend _____. I dreamed that he died and went to heaven. But in the dream the way to heaven was to climb a ladder. And as anyone climbed the ladder he was supposed to take a piece of chalk and make a mark on each rung for each sin he had committed.

As I looked in my dream, I saw _____ coming down the ladder. I asked him what he was doing. He said he was coming down for more chalk.

∽

Clergyman: someone who still preaches against modern dress even though there's not enough left to talk about.

CLOVERLEAF

California's state flower.

COINCIDENCE

Harry: What does coincidence mean?
Larry: Funny, I was going to ask you that same question.

COLD CUTS

Someone should press the "down" button on his elevator shoes.

∽

She's tried to get a man, but without avail—maybe she'd better wear one.

∽

Every girl has the right to be ugly, but she abused the privilege.

∽

She will never live to be as old as she looks.

∽

She looks like a million . . . every year of it.

∽

She has black hair and nails to match.

∽

Did you notice her cute little nose . . . the way it turned up, then down, then sideways?

∽

She looks like a professional blind date.

∽

His left eye was so fascinating that his right eye kept looking at it all the time.

∽

She has everything a man would desire—including heft, bulging muscles, and a moustache.

∽

The only thing that can make her look good is distance.

∾

Is that your nose, or are your eating a banana?

∾

Her hat looks as if it had made a forced landing on her head.

∾

She has worn that dress so many years it's been in style five times.

∾

Sit down; you make the place look shabby!

∾

He dresses like an unmade bed!

∾

That dress she's wearing will never go out of style . . . it will look just as ridiculous year after year.

∾

She has absolutely nothing to wear—and three closets to keep it in.

∾

She says that whenever she's down in the dumps she gets a new hat . . . I thought all along that's where she gets them.

∾

You were here last year, weren't you? I never forget a dress!

∾

You know, mister, you have some very funny material . . . in your suit!

❧

Don't try and judge her by her clothes . . . there isn't enough evidence.

❧

That's a very cute dress she almost has on.

❧

After they made him they broke the jelly mold.

❧

He has a great labor-saving device . . . tomorrow.

❧

She has a suit for every day of the month . . . the one she has on.

❧

Her clothes look as though she'd dressed in front of an airplane propeller.

❧

He's never been married . . . he's a self-made mouse.

❧

He is so nervous that he keeps coffee awake.

❧

He's the real decisive type . . . he'll give you a definite "maybe."

❧

They call him "Jigsaw." Every time he's faced with a problem he goes to pieces.

∽

Pardon my bluntness, but would you please stand down wind?

∽

She's a vision . . . a real sight.

∽

After her wedding everybody kissed the groom.

∽

When she comes into a room the mice jump on chairs.

∽

She's so ugly that when she goes to the beach the tide won't come in.

∽

He's a good argument for evolution . . . the missing link!

∽

Whatever is eating him must be suffering from indigestion.

∽

He's a contact man . . . all con and no tact.

∽

If he had his conscience taken out, it would be a minor operation.

∽

She puts her makeup on with a paint roller.

✌

In the etiquette class he once attended, he was unanimously voted the student most likely to return.

✌

I once saw a movie that was so bad six states use it in place of capital punishment.

✌

He left his job because of illness and fatigue . . . his boss got sick and tired of him.

✌

The only thing he's ever achieved on his own is dandruff.

✌

Why don't you get yourself x-rayed to see what people see in you.

✌

Next time you pass my house I'll appreciate it.

✌

They call him "Coliseum" . . . he's a monumental ruin.

✌

You've heard of the March of Time? This is his brother, Waste of Time!

✌

Anything goes tonight and you may be the first.

∽

He's full of brotherly love; he always stops anyone who's beating a donkey.

∽

Was the ground cold when you crawled out this morning?

∽

She has the knack of making strangers immediately.

∽

Just because you're a Democrat doesn't mean you're odd or obnoxious . . . stupid, maybe, but not odd or obnoxious.

∽

That's okay, folks . . . let him have his fun tonight. Tomorrow he'll be back on the garage truck.

∽

I understand when you were a kid your mother sent your picture to Ripley and it was promptly returned marked, "I don't believe it!"

∽

Let me just say, I've seen more excitement at the opening of an umbrella.

∽

Let me sum up this motion picture by saying, I've seen better film on teeth!

∽

I remember you . . . you're a graduate of the Don Rickles Charm School!

∽

That's very good. We ought to team up and do a single!

∽

Some cause happiness wherever they go; others, whenever they go.

∽

He says he'd only marry a girl who can take a joke . . . that's the only kind who would take him.

∽

Listen, baboon, don't accuse me of making a monkey out of you; why should I take all the credit?

∽

He's the kind of guy that can really creep into your heart and mind. In fact, you'll never meet a bigger creep!

∽

He looks like his mother was frightened by everything!

∽

When he was two, his family moved. But he found them again!

∽

Put your hand in front of your mouth when you sneeze. It keeps your teeth from flying out.

∽

It may just be morbid curiosity, but I would like to see your parents!

∽

When she goes down to the waterfront, even the tugboats stop whistling.

∽

He had to see his doctor in the morning for a blood test, so he stayed up all night studying for it.

∽

At a holiday party, they hung her and kissed the mistletoe.

∽

Guys like him don't grow on trees . . . they swing from them!

∽

He's a college man. You've heard of the rambling wrecks from Georgia Tech? Well, he's sort of a total loss from Holy Cross.

∽

Someday he'll be arrested for impersonating a human being!

∽

She has delusions of glamour!

∽

And just when did you fall out of the hearse?

∽

It's not the ups and downs in life that bother me, it's the jerks like you.

∽

He's one person who would make a perfect stranger!

∽

Stay with me . . . I want to be alone.

∽

Don't go away . . . I want to forget you exactly as you are.

∽

If you were alive, you'd be a very sick man.

∽

At almost every party his wife is sure to be asked by someone, "What does your husband want to be when he grows up?"

∽

When he leaves a party, the guests know the meaning of comic relief.

∽

They call him "garbage man" . . . he has a certain air about him.

∽

You remind me of some of those dances . . . one, two, three, jerk!

∽

I'd like to say we're glad you're here. I'd like to say it.

∽

I'll bet your parents hit the jerkpot.

∽

My son was annoying me the other morning, so I said, "Why don't you go out and play on the freeway?"

∽

I remember the day I had a wreck in my car. Six months later I married her.

∽

I had a girl that got so tan in the summer that I gave her a very practical birthday gift . . . saddle soap.

∽

She can't cook or clean but she can lick her weight in trading stamps.

∽

She made him a millionaire. Before she married him, he was a billionaire.

∽

I was invited up to Judy's place for dinner last night. I don't want to say she's a bad housekeeper, but you wipe your feet after you leave.

∽

He can stay longer in an hour than most people do in a week.

∽

When it comes to telling her age, she's shy . . . about ten years shy.

∽

He's a great athlete . . . he can throw a wet blanket the entire length of a room.

❧

He's a man of promise . . . broken promise.

❧

He lights up a room when he leaves it.

❧

There's no doubt he's trying . . . in fact, he's very trying.

❧

He's very cultured . . . he can bore you on any subject.

❧

He stopped drinking coffee in the morning because it keeps him awake the rest of the day.

❧

She's not completely useless: five charm schools are using her as a bad example.

❧

He's a real big gun . . . of small caliber and immense bore.

❧

Don't tell me . . . I know who you are. You're the reason for birth control.

❧

I understand you throw yourself into everything you undertake; please go and dig a deep well.

∽

They call her "Appendix" . . . if you take her out once, that's enough.

∽

He's mean, selfish, loudmouthed, and uncouth, but in spite of all that there's something about him that repels you.

∽

He claims he used to be an organist but gave it up . . . his money must have died.

∽

He's such a phony that he gets cavities in his false teeth.

∽

He was a born mountaineer and hasn't been on the level since.

∽

He has a face like a saint . . . a Saint Bernard.

∽

She has a face that looks like it wore out six bodies.

∽

She's had so many face-lifting jobs, every time she raises her eyebrows, she pulls up her stockings.

∽

I'm really pleased to see you're back . . . particularly after seeing your face.

∾

Well, well, well . . . all dressed up and no face to go.

∾

I never forget a face, but in your case, I'm willing to make an exception.

∾

There are two things I don't like about you . . . your face!

∾

She has a nice, open face . . . open day and night.

∾

I don't recall your face but your breath is familiar!

∾

Of course I'm listening to you; don't you see me yawning?

∾

I think you're the greatest, but then again, what do I know?

∾

"Some boys think I'm pretty and some think I'm ugly. What do you think?"
"A bit of both."

∾

His breath was so bad that his dentist had to work on his teeth through his ear.

∽

She's a rag, a bone, and a hank of hair—and he's a brag, a groan, and a tank of air.

COLLECTION PLATE

A minister was asked to inform a man with a heart condition that he had just inherited a million dollars. Everyone was afraid the shock would cause a heart attack and the man would die.

The minister went to the man's house and said, "Joe, what would you do if you inherited a million dollars?" Joe responded, "Well, Pastor, I think I would give half of it to the church."

The minister fell over dead.

∽

Someone asked, "What is the most sensitive nerve in the human body?"

The preacher answered, "The one that leads to the pocketbook."

∽

An artist was asked to contribute to a church fund drive. "I'm sorry, but I'm broke," he explained, "but I'll contribute a $400 picture."

The drive was almost complete when the minister came back to the artist. "We are still short $100 for the fund drive. Could you please help?"

"Of course," said the artist. "I'll increase the price of my picture to $500."

∽

A millionaire who had been bad all of his life was nearing the end of his time on earth and wanted to wipe the slate clean. To make amends for his evil ways, he donated a lot of money to a local church and had a meeting with the minister to discuss the possibility of getting into heaven.

Since the man had spent most of his life being evil, the minister couldn't really assure him he'd get into heaven, but he didn't want to disappoint the man and lose a big donation. Being diplomatic, the minister sized up the millionaire's chances like this:

"Mr. Jones, when it comes to riding on the heavenly railroad, think of yourself as a standby passenger."

COLLEGE

"I don't think we'll do too bad," said the student to the professor, referring to an upcoming football game.

The professor chided him for his bad grammar, pointing out that he should have said badly.

"Oh," said the student, "what difference does an 'ly' make?"

"Well," said the professor, "suppose you see a girl coming down the street. It makes a difference whether you look at her stern, or sternly."

∽

There's one great thing to be said for a college education. It enables you to worry about things all over the world.

∽

Friend: Has your son's education proved valuable?
Father: Yes, it has. It has cured his mother of bragging about him.

∽

A young college student wrote home to his family: "Dear Mom and Dad, I haven't heard from you in nearly a month. Please send a check so I'll know you're all right."

∽

Coed: Daddy, the girl who sits next to me in class has a dress just like mine.

Dad: So you want a new dress.
Coed: Well, it would be cheaper than changing colleges.

∾

A college education seldom hurts a man if he is willing to learn a little something after he graduates.

∾

You can tell a freshman,
by his slaphappy look.
You can tell a sophomore,
because he carries a comic book.
You can tell a junior,
by his debonairness and such.
You can tell a senior,
but you can't tell him much.

∾

A college boy said to his mother, "I decided that I want to be a political science major and that I want to clean up the mess in the world!"

"That's very nice," purred his mother. "You can go upstairs and start with your room."

∾

Father: Did you learn the three R's at college?
Son: You bet. Rah! Rah! Rah!

∾

The absent-minded professor of biology said to his class: "I have in this sack an excellent specimen of a frog that I dissected."

When he opened the sack he pulled out a sandwich and a cupcake. "Strange," he said, "I think I have already eaten lunch."

∾

Father: My son was a four-letter man in college.
Friend: Really?
Father: Yeah, D-U-M-B.

COMMERCIAL

A minister asked a little girl what she thought of her first church service. "The music was nice," she said, "but the commercial was too long."

COMMITTEE

A committee is a group of the unprepared, appointed by the unwilling, to do the unnecessary.

CONCLUSION

The troops were being taught to jump from a plane.
"What if my parachute doesn't open?" asked one rookie.
"That," said the instructor, "is known as jumping to a conclusion."

CONTRARY

She's so contrary that if she drowned they'd look upstream for her.

COOKING

Wife: Look at the old clothes I have to wear. If anyone came to visit, they would think I was the cook!
Husband: Well, they'd change their minds if they stayed for dinner!

ॐ

Wife one: Does your husband kick about his meals?
Wife two: No. What he kicks about is having to get them.

ॐ

: That is a beautiful turkey for Thanksgiving! What kind of stuffing did you use?
Wife: This one wasn't hollow!

⌒

Wife: Darling, you know that cake you asked me to bake for you? Well, the dog ate it.
Husband: That's okay, dear; don't cry. I'll buy you another dog.

⌒

When we first married, my wife was not a very good cook. She would make new desserts and have me try them before dinner.

One day I came home and she told me that she had just made a pumpkin pie. She told me to try some. I said, "How about after dinner?"

She said, "No, I want you to try it now."

I don't want to say it was bad, but I had to drink four glassfuls!

⌒

Wife: I baked two kinds of cookies today. Would you like to take your pick?
Husband: No thanks. I'll use my hammer.

⌒

Wife: This is rabbit stew we're having.
Husband: Thought so. I just found a hair in mine.

COURT

A lawyer was questioning the testimony of a witness to a shooting. "Did you see the shot fired?"

"No, sir, I only heard it."

"Stand down," said the judge sharply. "Your testimony is of no value."

The witness turned around in the box to leave, and when his back was turned to the judge he laughed loudly and derisively. Irate at this exhibition of contempt, the judge called the witness back to the chair and demanded to know how he dared to laugh at the court.

"Did you see me laugh, Judge?" asked the witness.

"No, but I heard you," retorted the judge.

"That evidence is not satisfactory, Your Honor," said the witness respectfully.

∽

Counsel: Do you wish to challenge any of the jury?

Prisoner: Well, I think I could lick that little fellow on this end.

∽

Judge: Guilty or not guilty?

Prisoner: Not guilty.

Judge: Have you ever been to prison before?

Prisoner: No, this is the first time I have stolen anything.

∽

Judge: Gentlemen of the jury, have you come to a decision?

Foreman: We have, Your Honor. The jury is all of the same mind—temporarily insane.

∽

"You have known the defendant how long?"

"Twelve years."

"Tell the court whether you think he is the type of man who would steal this money or not."

"How much was it?"

∽

A Chinese description of American court trials: "One man is silent, another talks all the time, and twelve wise men condemn the man who has not said a word."

∽

Judge: Haven't I seen you before?
Man: Yes, Your Honor. I taught your daughter how to play the piano.
Judge: Thirty years.

∽

Judge: Have you anything to offer the court before sentence is passed upon you?
Prisoner: No, Your Honor. My lawyer took my last dollar.

CRAZY

Psychiatrist: Congratulations, sir, you're cured.
Patient: Some cure. Before I was Julius Caesar. Now I'm nobody.

∽

"To tell the truth, Doctor," said a hardworking housewife, "I've always wanted to have a nervous breakdown. But every time I was about to get around to it, it was time to fix somebody a meal."

∽

Patient: Doctor, I think I'm a bridge.
Doctor: What on earth's come over you?
Patient: So far, ten cars, three buses and a truck.

∽

Patient: I went to a psychiatrist for six months. I thought I was a dog.
Friend: Well, did you get some help?
Patient: I sure did. I feel great now. Just feel my nose.

∽

Patient: I think I'm a slice of bread.
Doctor: You'll have to stop loafing around.

∽

The sad, quiet, big-eyed little lady sat in the psychiatrist's office. The good doctor questioned her gently as to why her family wanted her locked up.

"Now, tell me," he said, "just what your trouble is."

"It's just that . . . just that I'm so fond of pancakes, Doctor."

"Is that all? Why, I'm very fond of pancakes myself."

"Oh Doctor, really? You must come over to our house. I've got trunks and trunks full of them!"

A man mistook an insane asylum for a college. When his error was pointed out to him he said to the attendant, "Well, I don't suppose there's much difference."

"There's a big difference, Mister," said the attendant. "Here you have to show improvement before you get out."

Visitor: Why are you here?

Insane patient: For no reason at all.

"I've stopped going to the psychiatrist. He told me this morning that I was in love with my handbag."

"That's ridiculous!"

"I know. I mean, we're very fond of each other, but love?"

Patient: Doctor, I think that there are two of me.

Doctor: Why don't you both sit down and one of you tell me about it.

Patient: You see, Doctor, I have this habit of collecting spaghetti. My entire living room is filled with it.

Psychiatrist: Why don't you put it in the closet?

Patient: There's no room. That's where I keep the meatballs.

CRIME

Warden: I'm sorry. I find that we have kept you here a week too long.
Convict: That's all right, sir. Knock it off the next time.

CUFF LINKS

For my birthday my wife gave me three sets of cuff links. The only
trouble is that I do not have shirts with French cuffs. So I had to have
my wrists pierced.

CUPID

Cupid's dart hurt more coming out than going in.

CURRENCY

A substance which isn't current enough.

CZECHOSLOVAKIAN MIDGET

A Czechoslovakian midget was running through the side streets, trying to escape the secret police. At last he came to a small cafe and rapped
on the door.

"I know it's late," he said to the astonished proprietor. "But do you
suppose you could cache a small Czech?"

DAMP

Pam: Why was your letter so damp?
Rosie: Postage due, I guess.

DANIEL WEBSTER

Daniel Webster was once bested by one of the farmers of his native state. He had been hunting at some distance from his inn, and rather than make the long trip back, he approached a farmhouse some considerable time after dark and pounded on the door. An upstairs window was raised and the farmer, with head thrust out, called, "What do you want?"

"I want to spend the night here," said Webster.

"All right. Stay there," said the farmer. Down went the window.

DEACON

A Baptist deacon had advertised a cow for sale.

"How much are you asking for it?" inquired a prospective purchaser.

"A hundred and fifty dollars," said the advertiser.

"And how much mile does she give?"

"Four gallons a day," he replied.

"But how do I know that she will actually give that amount?" asked the purchaser.

"Oh, you can trust me," reassured the advertiser. "I'm a Baptist deacon."

"I'll buy it," replied the other. "I'll take the cow home and bring you back the money later. You can trust me; I'm a Presbyterian elder."

When the deacon arrived home he asked his wife, "What is a Presbyterian elder?"

"Oh," she explained, "a Presbyterian elder is about the same as a Baptist deacon."

"Oh, dear," groaned the deacon, "I have just lost my cow!"

Pastor: Say, deacon, a mule died out in front of the church.

Deacon: Well, it's the job of you ministers to look after the dead. Why tell me?

Pastor: You're right; it is my job. But we always notify the next of kin.

DEADBEAT

A doctor spotted a deadbeat patient while he was out to dinner. He called the patient aside and reminded him that he owed $250 for the work done more than two years earlier. He insisted that the man pay up. To the doctor's astonishment, the patient pulled a checkbook from his pocket and wrote a check to the doctor for the full amount.

Skeptical about the man's good faith, the doctor went directly to the bank the next morning and presented the check for payment. The teller handed back the check with the explanation that the patient's account was $25 short of the amount of the check. The doctor smiled, stepped back to the customer desk for a few minutes, came back to the teller, deposited $35 to the account of his former patient, and then again presented the $250 check. He walked out with a net gain of $215.

DEAL

A farmer and his wife went to a fair. The farmer was fascinated by the airplane rides, but he balked at the $10 tickets.

"Let's make a deal," said the pilot. "If you and your wife can ride without making a single sound, I won't charge you anything. Otherwise you pay the $10."

"Good deal!" said the farmer.

So they went for a ride. When they got back the pilot said, "If I hadn't been there, I never would have believed it. You never made a sound!"

"It wasn't easy, either," said the farmer. "I almost yelled when my wife fell out."

DEBT

"Thankful! What have I to be thankful for? I can't pay any of my bills!"

"Then, be thankful you aren't one of the creditors."

Why is it that every time you start to make ends meet, somebody comes along and moves the ends?

❧

A customer was several months behind in paying his bill, and his last payment notice informed him that he would have to pay or the matter would be turned over to a lawyer. He responded with the following note: "Enclosed you will find a check for the entire amount. Please forgive my delay in not answering sooner. Thank you for your patience. I remain, Yours truly . . ."

"P.S. This is the kind of a letter I would write to you if I had the money to pay."

❧

The man had barely paid off the mortgage on his house when he mortgaged it again to buy a car and, not long after, he borrowed to build a garage. His banker hesitated and said, "If I do make this new loan, how will you buy gas for the car?"

"It seems to me," replied the borrower curtly, "that a fellow who owns a big house, a car, and a garage should be able to get credit for gasoline."

❧

"I can't pay the rent this month."
"But you said that last month."
"I kept my word, didn't I?"

❧

Shopper: "The way food prices are going up, it soon will be cheaper to eat the money."

DEMOCRATS

The rumor was started that the Democrats were against religion and for atheism. In fact, they might even destroy the Bible.

An old lady, wondering how the Scriptures could be preserved in such an event, called on a Democrat friend in her town and asked him to hide her Bible.

After scoffing at the idea that Democrats would suppress and destroy all the Bibles, the Democrat asked the old lady why she wanted him to hide her Bible.

"Because," she said, "they'll never think of looking for a Bible in the house of a Democrat."

❦

The Southern father was introducing his family of boys to a visiting governor.

"Thirteen boys," exclaimed the governor, "and all Democrats, I suppose."

"All but one," said the father proudly. "They're all Democrats but Willie, the little rascal. He got to readin'."

❦

I never said all Democrats were saloonkeepers; what I said was all saloonkeepers were Democrats.

DENOMINATOR

Son: Dad, will you help me find the least common denominator in this problem?

Dad: Good heavens, son, don't tell me that hasn't been found. They were looking for it when I was a kid.

DENTIST

Ryan: Did you hear about the dentist who married the manicurist?
Bryan: No, I didn't.
Ryan: It didn't last. After a month they were fighting tooth and nail.

❦

Dentist: What kind of filling would you like in your tooth?
Boy: Chocolate!

❦

Mrs. Williams wasn't very happy about having her tooth pulled, but the dentist assured her there was no other choice. Nonetheless, every time he went to put the forceps in her mouth, she clenched her teeth.

Whispering to the nurse, the dentist tried again. At the instant he approached her, the nurse pinched Mrs. Williams on the bottom with all her strength. The woman's mouth opened wide, and the tooth was pulled.

"Now," the dentist said when it was all over, "that wasn't so bad."

"No," Mrs. Williams agreed. "But who would have imagined that the roots went so far down!"

∽

There are three basic rules for having good teeth:
1. Brush them twice a day.
2. See your dentist twice a year.
3. Keep your nose out of other people's business.

∽

Patient: Hey, that wasn't the tooth I wanted pulled.
Dentist: Calm yourself, I'm coming to it!

DEODORANT

Joe: What are you doing with those two pillows under your arms?
Moe: These aren't pillows. They are five-year deodorant pads!

DIAMOND RING

Mr. Smith bought a beautiful diamond ring for his wife and at lunch showed it to his friend Mr. Jones. Jones offered to buy it for more than Smith had paid. Smith later regretted the sale and bought it back from Jones at a still higher price, but Jones again bought it back from Smith at a much higher price. Finally Jones sold the ring to a person unknown to Smith.

When Smith heard of this final transaction he protested. "How could you do such a stupid thing!" he said. "That was crazy. We were both making such a good living from that ring!"

DILLY

Now for a couple of dillies: DILLY, DILLY.

DIPHTHERIA

Mary: Are you every troubled with diphtheria?
Sally: Only when I try to spell it.

DISAGREE

Wife: I'm afraid the mountain air would disagree with me.
Husband: My dear, it wouldn't dare.

DISHES

Wife: Would you help me with the dishes?
Husband: That isn't a man's job.
Wife: The Bible suggests that it is.
Husband: Where does it say that?
Wife: In 2 Kings 21:13 it says, "I will wipe Jerusalem as a man wipeth a dish; wiping it, and turning it upside down."

DO-IT-YOURSELF

He's a do-it-yourself man. He made a bay window with a knife and fork.

DOCTOR

Patient: Doctor, how can I broaden my mind?
Doctor: How about a stick of dynamite between your ears?

A doctor had a problem with a leak in his bathroom plumbing that became bigger and bigger. Even though it was 2 A.M., the doctor decided to phone his plumber.

"For Pete's sake, Doc," he wailed, "this is some time to wake a guy."

"Well," the doctor answered testily, "you've never hesitated to call me in the middle of the night with a medical problem. Now it just happens I've got a plumbing emergency."

There was a moment's silence. Then the plumber spoke up. "Right you are, Doc," he agreed. "Tell me what's wrong."

The doctor explained about the leak in the bathroom.

"Tell you what to do," the plumber offered. "Take two aspirins every four hours and drop them down the pipe. If the lead hasn't cleared up by morning, phone me at the office."

☙

Medical Student: There's something written on this patient's foot.
Doctor: That's right. It's a footnote.

☙

Did you hear about the man who complained that every time he put on his hat he heard music? The doctor fixed him up: He removed his hatband.

☙

The nurse burst into the doctor's office. "Dr. Poure!" she yelled. "You just gave Mr. Weston a clean bill of health . . . and he dropped dead right outside the door on his way out."

Dr. Poure leaped into action. "Quick," he said. "We've got to turn him around so it looks like he was just coming in."

☙

Patient: Doctor, I keep seeing frogs in front of my eyes.
Doctor: Don't worry. It's only a hoptical illusion.

☙

A lady complained of an earache, so the doctor examined her and found a piece of string dangling from her right ear. The doctor began pulling it out, and the more he pulled, the more string came out. Suddenly the pulling became harder, and he struggled with the string. To his amazement, out fell a bouquet of roses.

The doctor exclaimed, "Good gracious, where did this come from?"

"How should I know?" said the patient. "Why don't you look at the card?"

∽

A lady with a bad rash visited a dermatologist. It was the type of condition that had been present for some time.

"Have you been treated for this rash before?" inquired the doctor.

"Yes, by my druggist."

"And what sort of foolish advice did he give you?" asked the doctor.

"Oh, he told me to come and see you."

∽

Doctor: There goes the only woman I ever loved.
Nurse: Why don't you marry her?
Doctor: I can't afford to. She's my best patient.

∽

Stranger: Good morning, Doctor. I just dropped in to tell you how much I benefited from your treatment.
Doctor: But you're not one of my patients.
Stranger: I know. But my Uncle Bill was, and I'm his heir.

∽

"Doctor, will I be able to read with these new glasses?"
"Yes, of course."
"Good! I never could read before."

∽

He is a very fine doctor. If you can't afford the operation, he touches up the x-rays.

∽

Doctor: I have some good news and some bad news. Which do you want first?
Patient: Give me the bad news first.
Doctor: We amputated the wrong leg.
Patient: What is the good news?
Doctor: Your other leg won't need to be amputated after all.

∽

Mrs. Jones was suddenly ill in the night, and a new doctor was called. After a look at the patient, the doctor stepped outside the sickroom to ask Mr. Jones for a corkscrew. Given the tool, he disappeared but several minutes later was back demanding a pair of pliers. Again he disappeared into the room of the moaning patient, only to call out again, "A chisel and a mallet, quickly."
Mr. Jones could stand it no longer. "What is her trouble, doctor?"
"Don't know yet," was the reply. "Can't get my instrument bag open."

∽

I went to my doctor last week and he told me to take a hot bath before retiring. But that's ridiculous! It'll be years before I retire!

∽

A doctor, appearing as an expert witness on behalf of a man injured in a car accident, was being badgered by an overbearing attorney.
"You say, Doctor, that you're familiar with the symptoms of a brain concussion?"
"That's correct," replied the doctor.
"Well tell me, Doctor," continued the attorney, "if you and I were riding in a car and another car struck us and our heads bumped together, is it your opinion that we would suffer a concussion?"
"It's my opinion," replied the doctor, "that I would and you wouldn't."

∽

Doctors say that if you eat slowly you eat less. You certainly will if you are a member of a large family.

Doctors' Bills

Patient one: How many doctors does it take to screw in a lightbulb?
Patient two: How many?
Patient one: It depends on whether or not the bulb has health insurance.

∽

Patient: Doctor, it's 2 A.M. and I can't sleep; it is the bill I owe you. I can't pay it. It bothers me so much I can't sleep.
Doctor: Why did you have to tell me that? Now I can't sleep.

∽

Doctor: Say, the check you gave me for my bill came back.
Patient: So did my arthritis!

∽

Patient: Doc, am I getting better?
Doctor: I don't know—let me feel your purse.

∽

Consultation: A medical term meaning "share the wealth."

Dog

When Joe was a little boy, he took fiddle lessons. One day while he was practicing, scraping dismally back and forth with his bow, his dog set up a plaintive wailing and howling. Finally Joan, who was trying to do her homework, stuck her head into the room where her brother was practicing.

"For goodness sake!" she complained. "Can't you play something the dog doesn't know?"

∽

Mark: What is the name of your dog?
Ryan: Ginger.
Mark: Does Ginger bite?
Ryan: No, but Ginger snaps.

❦

Bob: Don't be afraid of my dog. You know the old proverb, "A barking dog never bites."
Rich: Yes, you know the proverb, and I know the proverb, but does your dog know the proverb?

❦

Bill: My dog swallowed a tapeworm and died by inches.
Bob: That's nothing—my dog crawled up in my bed and died by the foot.
Ken: I can beat that. I had a dog that went out of the house and died by the yard.

❦

Q: If a dog lost his tail, where would he get another one?
A: At the retail store, naturally.

❦

A man dropped in to pay a friend an unexpected visit, and was amazed to find him playing chess with a dog. The man watched in silence for a few minutes, then burst with, "That's the most incredible dog I ever saw in my life!"

"Oh, he isn't so smart," the friend answered. "I've beaten him three games out of four."

DREAM HOUSE

We've just moved into our dream house. It costs twice as much as we ever dreamed it would.

Drive-in Confessional

Have you heard of the new drive-in confessional? It is called "Toot and Tell!"

Druggist

So this druggist is filling a prescription, hands his customer a little bottle with twelve pills in it, and says, "That'll be $4.50." Suddenly the phone rings and as the druggist turns to answer it, the customer puts 50¢ on the counter, walks out. The druggist turns back, spots the 50¢ and yells: "Sir! Sir! That's $4.50, not 50¢. Sir!" The guy is gone. The druggist picks up the half a buck, looks at it, shrugs, flips it into the till, and mumbles, "Oh, well, 40¢ profit is better than nothing."

Dull

Bore: I shot this lion in Africa. It was a case of him or me.
Bored: Well, the lion certainly makes a better rug.

∽

A bore is someone who goes on talking while you're interrupting.

Dumb Question

"Did you fall down the elevator shaft?"
"No, I was sitting here and they built it around me."

Dunlap's Disease

"He is suffering from Dunlap's disease."
"What is Dunlap's disease?"
"His stomach done-laps over his belt!"

☙ E ☙

ECCENTRICS

Wife: Everyone is talking about the Carlsons' quarrel. Some people are taking his side and others are taking her side.

Husband: And I suppose a few eccentrics are minding their own business.

EGRESS

It is said that Phineas T. Barnum, the famed circus magnate, hung a large sign over one of the exits of his museum which read, "This way to the egress." Many people in the crowds, eager to see what an egress looked like, passed through the door and found themselves out on the street.

ELECTRIC BLANKET

Husband: How do you want the electric blanket tonight, dear . . . rare, medium, or well done?

ELEPHANT

Tom: Do you know how to get down from an elephant?

Jerry: No.

Tom: You don't get down from an elephant; you get down from a duck.

☙

Q: Why do elephants have flat feet?

A: From jumping out of trees.

☙

Q: Why is it dangerous to go into the jungle between two and four in the afternoon?
A: Because that's when elephants are jumping out of trees.

∽

Q: Why are pygmies so small?
A: They went into the jungle between two and four in the afternoon.

∽

Pat: I can lift an elephant with one hand.
Matt: That's impossible.
Pat: No, it's not. Find me an elephant with one hand and I'll prove it.

∽

Harry: What do you get when you cross an elephant and a mouse?
Cary: I don't know.
Harry: I don't know either, but it sure makes big holes in the walls.

∽

Q: How do you make an elephant fly?
A: Well, first you take a grea-a-t big zipper . . .

∽

Joe: What did the banana say to the elephant?
Moe: I don't know.
Joe: Nothing. Bananas can't talk.

ELEPHANT'S EAR SANDWICH

Customer: Your sign says, "$50 to anyone who orders something we can't furnish." I would like to have an elephant ear sandwich.
Waiter: Ohhh . . . we're going to have to pay you the $50.
Customer: No elephant ears, huh?
Waiter: Oh, we've got lots of them . . . but we're all out of those big buns!

ENGAGEMENT RING

He: Here is your engagement ring.
She: But this diamond has a flaw in it.
He: You shouldn't notice that—we are in love and love is blind.
She: Not stone blind.

EPISTLE

Sunday school teacher: What are Epistles?
Student: I guess they are the wives of the Apostles.

EVERYDAY FACE

The popular preacher Charles Spurgeon was admonishing a class of divinity students on the importance of making the facial expressions harmonize with the speech in delivering sermons. "When you speak of heaven," he said, "let your face light up and be irradiated with a heavenly gleam. Let your eyes shine with reflected glory. And when you speak of hell . . . well, then your everyday face will do."

EXCUSES

In order to take care of all the excuses for not attending church, the following information was placed in a local newspaper:

1. Beds will be placed in the fellowship hall for those who say, "Sunday is my only day to rest."

2. Eye drops will be available for those with tired eyes from watching TV too late on Saturday night.

3. Steel helmets will be provided for those who say, "The roof would cave in if I ever went to church."

4. Blankets will be furnished for those who think that church is too cold and air-conditioning for those who say that it is too hot.

5. We will reserve the front pews for those who like the pastor's sermons and the back pews with earplugs for those who dislike his sermons.

6. Scorecards will be available for those who list the hypocrites present.

7. TV dinners will be available for those who can't go to church and cook the noon meal for the family.

8. We will have a selection of trees and shrubs for those who like to see God in nature.

EYE

Policeman: I'm looking for a man with one eye named Carnell.
Bystander: What's his other eye called?

EYE SORE

"Every time I have a cup of coffee, I get a stabbing pain in my right eye. What shall I do?"
"Take the spoon out of your cup."

FAINTED

A man rose from his seat in a crowded bus so a lady standing nearby could sit down. She was so surprised she fainted.

When she revived and sat down, she said, "Thanks." Then he fainted.

FALLS

Did you hear about the man who jumped from the Empire State Building and lived to tell about it? He told the people on the ninety-third floor, those on the eighty-fourth floor, everyone on the sixty-second floor, and those on . . .

⁓

Ken: My uncle fell off a scaffolding and was killed.
Bob: What was he doing up on the scaffolding?
Ken: Getting hanged.

FAMILY

A young mother asked her husband to take the two-year-old for a walk. The husband was busy working on a project, but with a deep sigh (the kind that let his wife know he was not pleased), he grabbed the baby carriage and began walking around the block in the hot sun.

"Honey," shouted the young mother from the second-story window.

"Leave me alone!" he called back. "We're all right."

An hour later his wife once again pleaded, "Honey."

"Well, what do you want?" he replied in a gruff way. "Is there anything wrong in the house?"

"No, honey," replied his wife. "But you've been wheeling little Suzie's doll all afternoon. Isn't it time for the baby to have a turn?"

⁓

Father calling to his daughter as her date waits: Dreamboat! Your barnacle is here!

∽

I think there is insanity in my family. They keep asking me for money.

FAMOUS LAST WORDS

"Just watch me dive from that bridge."

∽

"If you knew anything you wouldn't be a traffic cop."

∽

"Lemme have that bottle; I'll try it."

∽

"What? Your mother is going to stay another month?"

∽

"Say, who's boss of this joint, anyhow?"

FARMER

A farmer had a wife who was very critical of his vocabulary. One evening he told her he had a friend named Bill he would like for her to meet.
"Don't call him 'Bill,'" she insisted. "Call him 'William.'"
When the friend arrived, the farmer said, "Let me tell you a tale."
"Not tale," the wife interrupted. "Say, 'anecdote.'"
That night, upon retiring, the farmer told her to put out the light.
"Not 'put out,'" she exclaimed. "Say, 'extinguish' the light."
Later in the night she awakened her husband and sent him downstairs to investigate a noise. When he returned, she asked him what it was.

"It was," he explained carefully, "a William goat which I took by its anecdote and extinguished."

❧

A farmer vows he increased egg production by putting this sign in the henhouse: "An egg a day keeps Colonel Sanders away."

❧

City Slicker: Look at that bunch of cows.
Farmer: Not bunch . . . herd.
City Slicker: Heard what?
Farmer: Herd of cows.
City Slicker: Sure I've heard of cows.
Farmer: No, a cow herd.
City Slicker: Why should I care what a cow heard? I've no secrets from a cow.

❧

Farmer: Is this seed guaranteed?
Merchant: It certainly is. If the seed doesn't grow, just bring it back, and we'll refund the money.

❧

A farmer whose barn burned down was told by the insurance company that his policy provided that the company build a new barn, rather than paying him the cash value. The farmer was incensed by this. "If this is the way you fellows operate," he said, "then cancel the insurance I have on my wife's life."

FAULTS

"Once a friend of mine and I agreed it would be helpful for each of us to tell the other all our faults."
"How did it work?"
"We haven't spoken for five years."

❧

First man: I think we should all confess our faults one to another. I've got a terrible habit of stealing!

Second man: I've got a terrible habit of lying!

Third man: I beat my wife!

Fourth man: When no one is around, I get drunk!

Fifth man: I've got the terrible habit of gossiping, and I can hardly wait to get out of here!

FINGERS

My wife bawled me out for eating with my fingers. But I've always said that if food isn't clean enough to pick up with your fingers, it isn't fit to eat.

∽

Sister: Is it good manners to eat chicken with your fingers?

Brother: No, you should eat your fingers separately.

FISHING

Two men fishing on Sunday morning were feeling pretty guilty, especially since the fish didn't bite. One said to the other, "I guess I should have stayed home and gone to church."

To which the other angler replied lazily, "I couldn't have gone to church anyway. My wife's sick in bed."

∽

Once upon a time there was a fisherman who had two sons named Toward and Away. Every day he would go fishing and return late at night, always talking about the giant fish he had almost caught. One day he took Toward and Away fishing with him.

That night he returned home more excited than ever.

"Sally," he yelled to his wife, "you should have seen the fish I saw today. A tremendous gray fish, ten feet long with horns and fur all over its back. It had legs like a caterpillar. It came crawling out of the water, snatched our son Toward, and swallowed him in one gulp!"

"Good gracious!" exclaimed his wife. "That's horrible!"

"Oh, that was nothing," said her husband. "You should have seen the one that got Away!"

∽

The world would be a better place if all men showed as much patience as they do when they're waiting for a fish to bite.

∽

Red: Did you mark that place where the fishing was good?
Ted: Yes, I put an X on the side of the boat.
Red: That was stupid. What if we should take out another boat next time?

∽

"I caught a 250-pound marlin the other day!"
"That's nothing. I was fishing and hooked a lamp from an old Spanish ship. In fact, the light was still lit!"
"If you will blow out the light, I'll take 200 pounds off the marlin!"

∽

There were three men in a boat halfway across a lake. The first man suddenly said, "I forgot my lunch," got out of the boat, and walked to shore on top of the water.

Later, the second man said, "I forgot my fishing tackle," and also walked across the water to shore.

By this time, the third man thought to himself, "They're not going to outsmart me. I forgot my bait can," and he started to walk across the water, but he sank.

The first man said to the second, "Maybe we should have told him where the rocks were."

FLASHLIGHT

A boy from New York was being led through the swamps of Georgia.
"Is it true," he asked, "that an alligator won't attack you if you carry a flashlight?"

"That depends," replied the guide, "on how fast you carry the flashlight."

FOOD

Did you hear about the man who swallowed an unplucked goose? He felt a little down in the mouth.

∽

First man: I'm so hungry I could eat a horse.
Second man: I'm so hungry I could eat a moose.
Third Man: I'm so hungry I could eat a bear.
Woman: I've just lost my appetite.

FOOT

Moe: You're stepping on my foot. Why don't you put your foot where it belongs?
Joe: If I did, you'd go through the door.

FOREMAN

The news that Bill had lost his job got around quickly, and a friend asked, "Why did the foreman fire you?"
"You know that a foreman is . . ." Bill shrugged, "the one who stands around and watches the other men work."
"What's that got to do with it?" his friend wanted to know.
"Well, he just got jealous of me," Bill explained. "Everyone thought I was the foreman."

FORGETFUL

"George is so forgetful," the sales manager complained to his secretary. "It's a wonder he can sell anything. I asked him to pick me up some sandwiches on his way back from lunch, and I'm not sure he'll even remember to come back."

Just then the door flew open, and in bounced George. "You'll never guess what happened!" he shouted. "While I was at lunch, I met old man Brown, who hasn't bought anything from us for five years. Well, we got to talking and he gave me this half-million dollar order!"

"See," sighed the sales manager to his secretary, "I told you he'd forget the sandwiches."

GAMBLING

The trouble with hitting the jackpot on a slot machine is that it takes so long to put the money back in the machine.

⁓

The story is told of a corporal who reported to a new regiment with a letter from his old captain, saying, "This man is a great soldier, and he'll be even better if you can cure him of his constant gambling."

The new C.O. looked at him sternly and said, "I hear you're an inveterate gambler. I don't approve. It's bad for discipline. What kind of things do you bet on?"

"Practically anything, sir," said the corporal. "If you'd like, I'll bet you my next month's pay that you've got a strawberry birthmark under your right arm."

The C.O. snapped, "Put down your money." He then stripped to the waist, proved conclusively he had no birthmark, and pocketed the bills on the table. He couldn't wait to phone the captain and exult, "That corporal of yours won't be in a hurry to make a bet after what I just did to him."

"Don't be too sure," said the captain mournfully. "He just wagered me twenty to two hundred he'd get you to take your shirt off five minutes after he reported."

GARBAGE COLLECTION

If the garbage workers in your community ever go on strike, you might like to know how a wise New Yorker disposed of his refuse for the nine days the sanitation workers were off the job last summer. Each day he wrapped his garbage in gift paper, then he put it in a shopping bag. When he parked his car, he left the bag on the front seat with the window open. When he got back to the car, the garbage always had been collected.

⁓

I saw a hippie running after a garbage truck this morning, yelling, "Taxi! Taxi!"

Garden Tools

Wife to husband: Look, Ralph, the first garden tools are peeping their heads above the snow.

Gasoline

A boy and a girl were out driving one evening. They came to a quiet spot on a country lane, and the car stopped. "Out of gas," said the boy.
The girl opened her purse and pulled out a bottle.
"Wow!" said the boy. "A bottle . . . what is it?"
"Gasoline," said the girl.

Getting Married

A couple, just married, got among their wedding presents two tickets to a very fine show, with the notation "Guess who" on the tickets. They went to the play. When they returned, all of their wedding presents were gone, and a note was left also: "Now you know!"

❧

Father: Can you support her in the way she's been accustomed to?
Prospective son-in-law: No, perhaps I cannot support her in the manner she has been accustomed to, but I can support her in the way her mother was accustomed to when she was first married.

❧

"You know, girls, a lot of men are going to be miserable when I marry."
"Really? How many men are you going to marry?"

❧

"What would you say if I asked you to be my wife?"
"Nothing. I can't talk and laugh at the same time."

∽

Speaking about marriages of high school kids, one elderly gent of twenty swore he attended a wedding ceremony where the bridegroom wept for two hours. It seems the bride got a bigger piece of cake than he did.

∽

What a holler would ensue if people had to pay the minister as much to marry them as they have to pay a lawyer to get them a divorce.

∽

Mary: Well, what happened when you showed the girls in the office your new engagement ring? Did they all admire it?
Sara: Better than that, four of them recognized it.

∽

I just heard of a man who met his wife at a travel bureau. She was looking for a vacation and he was the last resort.

GLACIER

"Dear me," said the old lady on a visit to the mountains, "look at all those rocks. Where did they all come from?"
"The glaciers brought them down," said the guide.
"But where are the glaciers?"
"The glaciers," said the guide with a weary voice, "have gone back for more rocks."

GLASS EYE

Christy: That lady has a glass eye.
Lisa: How did you find that out?
Christy: Well, it just came out in the conversation.

GNU

Mama Gnu was waiting for Papa Gnu as he came home for dinner one evening. "Our little boy was very bad today," she declared. "I want you to punish him."

"Oh no," said Papa Gnu. "I won't punish him. You'll have to learn to paddle your own gnu."

GOLF

Golfer: Why do you keep looking at your watch?
Caddy: This isn't a watch, sir. It's a compass!

∾

Golfer: The doctor says I can't play golf.
Caddy: Ah, he's played with you, too, huh?

∾

"Caddy, why didn't you see where that ball went?"
"Well, it doesn't usually go anywhere, Mr. Smith. You got me off guard."

∾

Man to friend: After three sets of clubs and ten years of lessons, I'm finally getting some fun out of golf. I quit.

∾

Lady customer: I would like to buy a low handicap.
Sales clerk at sporting goods shop: A low handicap? I don't understand.
Lady customer: I want to give it to my husband for his birthday; he's always wishing for one.

∾

The other day I was playing golf and saw an unusual thing. A golfer became so mad that he threw his brand-new set of golf clubs into the lake. A few minutes later he came back, waded into the lake, and retrieved his clubs. He proceeded to take his car keys out of the bag and then threw the clubs back into the water.

༄

A group of golfers were telling tall stories. At last came a veteran's turn. "Well," he said, "I once drove a ball, accidentally of course, through a cottage window. The ball knocked over an oil lamp and the place caught on fire."

"What did you do?" asked his friends.

"Oh," said the veteran, "I immediately teed another ball, took careful aim, and hit the fire alarm on Main Street. That brought out the fire engine before any major damage was done."

༄

Yes, it is true. We have more golf curses per mile than anywhere else in the world.

༄

Mr. Hanson died on the golf course, and no one wanted to tell his wife the bad news. Finally a friend placed the call.

"Joan," he said, "Richard lost $5000 playing poker."

"What!" she screamed. "He should drop dead."

"Funny you should mention that. . . ."

༄

First golfer: What's your golf score?
Second golfer: Well, not so good. It's 72.
First golfer: That's not so bad. In fact, it's really good.
Second golfer: Well, I'm hoping I do better on the next hole.

༄

Golfer: Well, what do you think of my game?
Caddy: I guess it's all right, but I still like golf better.

༄

Golfer: How would you have played that last shot, caddy?
Caddy: Under an assumed name!

∽

Golfer: You must be the world's worst caddy!
Caddy: No, sir! That would be too much of a coincidence!

Good Luck

Bart: Did you hear what happened to the scientist who mixed poison ivy and a four-leaf clover?
Art: What happened?
Bart: He ended up with a rash of good luck.

Good News/Bad News

The loudspeaker of the big jet clicked on and the captain's voice announced in a clear, even tone: "Now there's no cause for alarm but we felt you passengers should know that for the last three hours we've been flying without the benefit of radio, compass, radar, or navigational beam due to the breakdown of certain key components. This means that we are, in the broad sense of the word, lost, and are not quite sure in which direction we are heading. I'm sure you'll be glad to know, however, on the brighter side of the picture, that we're making excellent time!"

∽

Bad news: Your wife just ran off with your best friend.
Good news: That's two people off your Christmas list.

∽

Good news: All of you slaves on the galley are going to get an extra-special ration of rum with the noon meal.
Bad news: After lunch, the captain wants to go waterskiing.

∽

Doctor: Would you like the good news or the bad news?
Patient: Give me the good news.
Doctor: You've only got three weeks to live.
Patient: If that's the good news, what's the bad news?
Doctor: I should have told you two weeks ago.

GOLD

A member of the Inca tribe was captured by the Spanish. The captain told his interpreter to say to the Inca Indian, "Tell him if he doesn't tell us where they have hidden all their gold, we will burn both of his feet in the fire."

Through the interpreter the Inca responded, "I'd rather die than tell you where the gold is." With that they burned his feet in the fire.

The captain then told the interpreter to say, "Tell him if he doesn't tell us where the gold is hidden, we will hang him from that noose on the tree over there."

The Inca again responded, "I'd rather die than tell you where the gold is." With that, they took him over to the tree and hanged him until he could hardly breathe.

The Spanish captain then ordered the Indian to be brought to him again. This time he said to the interpreter, "Tell him if he doesn't tell us where the gold is, we will skin him alive."

The Inca could stand it no longer and said, "The gold is hidden in a little cave just behind the large waterfall. The waterfall is one mile over the hill to the right."

The interpreter related the following to the captain, "He said that he would rather die than tell you where the gold is."

GOUT

A local minister was troubled by one of his members who was constantly drinking alcohol. They happened to run into each other at a shopping mall. The drinker came up to the minister and asked, "Pastor, what causes gout?"

The minister thought that this would be a good opportunity to admonish the man about his drinking. "It comes from drinking too much alcohol."

"Oh, I see," said the man. "I just read in the paper that the pope and the president were both suffering from gout."

GOVERNMENT

A fine is a tax for doing wrong. A tax is a fine for doing well.

ᡣᠣ

Governmental machinery is the marvelous device which enables ten men to do the work of one.

ᡣᠣ

Politician: I have nothing to say to the newspaper.
Reporter: I know that. Now let's get down to the interview.

GRASS HOUSES

Did you hear about the tribe in Africa that stole the king's throne from a rival tribe? They hid the throne in the rafters of their grass hut. The men who stole the throne were having a party in the hut. They were feeling happy about their successful theft when all of a sudden the rafters broke and the throne fell down and killed all of the men.
Moral: Those who live in grass houses shouldn't stow thrones.

GUARDIAN ANGEL

Wife: Aren't you driving a little too fast, dear?
Husband: Don't you believe in a guardian angel? He'll take care of us.
Wife: Yes, I do. But I'm afraid we left him miles back!

GUEST TOWELS

The most embarrassing moment in the life of Jane Wyman happened when she was entertaining very special guests. After looking over all the appointments carefully, she put a note on the guest towels: "If you use these I will murder you." It was meant for her husband. In the excitement she forgot to remove the note. After the guests departed, the towels were discovered still in perfect order, as well as the note itself.

H

HAIRCUT

I've got a sixteen-year-old son who was 6'3" until he got a haircut. Now he is 5'8".

∾

A long-haired boy was trying to get into a swim club, but was stopped by the owner who tried to explain that for health reasons long-haired boys were prohibited from using the pool.

"Get a haircut, and you're welcome," said the owner.

"Some of history's greatest men had long hair," said the young man.

"Those are the rules."

"Moses had long hair."

"Moses can't swim in our pool, either."

HAIRDO

We're constantly amazed at these young things with their fancy hair-dos and skintight pants. And the girls are even worse.

HAMMER FROM SEARS

A man was sitting in a cafe when all of a sudden someone came in and beat him up. When he woke up he said to the owner, "Who was that?"

"That was Kung Fu from China," replied the owner.

Next week the man was eating in the same cafe when a different person entered and beat him up. When he woke up he said to the owner, "Who was that?"

The owner said, "That was Kuang Chow from Taiwan."

Several weeks later Kung Fu and Kuang Chow were eating in the cafe. The man who had been beaten by both of them entered and did his work. He said to the owner, "When they wake, tell them that was a hammer from Sears."

HANDWRITING

Teacher: Really, Tommy, your handwriting is terrible! You must learn to write better.

Tommy: Well, if I did, you'd be finding fault with my spelling.

HAPPY ENDING

"Did the movie have a happy ending?"

"Yes, everyone was glad it was over."

HATCHET

There's no point in burying a hatchet if you're going to put up a marker on the site.

HEARING AID

Mark: I just purchased the most expensive hearing aid ever made. It is imported from Germany and is guaranteed for life.

Clark: How much did it cost?

Mark: Five past two.

HEAVEN AND HELL

St. Peter looked at the new arrival skeptically; he had no advance knowledge of his coming.

"How did you get here?" he asked.

"Flu."

∽

The devil challenged St. Peter to a baseball game. "How can you win, Satan?" asked St. Peter. "All the famous ballplayers are up here."

"How can I lose?" answered Satan. "All the umpires are down here."

∽

One day the gate between Heaven and Hell broke down, and Saint Peter and Satan got into a bitter dispute about whose responsibility it was to repair it. After much argument they could not arrive at an agreement. Then Saint Peter said he would hire a lawyer to defend the interests of Heaven.

"Where are you going to get a lawyer?" asked Satan. "I've got them all."

Heckler: I wouldn't vote for you if you were Saint Peter!
Politician: If I were Saint Peter you wouldn't be in my precinct.

She's an angel . . . always up in the air and harping on something.

Old Pete was very close to dying but made a miraculous recovery. In the hospital his pastor came to visit him and the conversation went like this:

"Tell me, Pete: When you were so near death's door, did you feel afraid to meet your Maker?"

"No, Pastor," said Peter. "It was the other man I was afraid of!"

Henpecked Husband

I have been married thirty-six years and I don't regret one day of it. The one unregrettable day was July 8, 1953.

First husband: Have you ever suspected your wife of leading a double life?
Second husband: Continually—her own and mine.

"Hello, Sam," exclaimed Jim, meeting a buddy for the first time since the war's end. "Did you marry that girl you used to go with or are you still doing your own cooking and ironing?"

"Yes," replied Sam.

∾

First husband: Well, I can tell you're a married man all right. No holes in your socks now.

Second husband: No. One of the first things my wife taught me was how to darn them.

∾

"Why are you so sad, Bill?"

"My wife said she wouldn't talk to me for thirty days."

"Why should that make you sad?"

"Today is her last day!"

∾

Announcement: The lodge meeting will be postponed. The Supreme Exalted Invincible Unlimited Sixty-Ninth Degree Potentate's wife wouldn't let him come!

∾

She refuses to give him a divorce. She says, "I've suffered with the bum for fifteen years, and now I should make him happy?"

∾

Husband overheard at a party muttering to his wife, "What did I say to offend you, dear? It might come in useful again sometime."

∾

The news media featured a convict's daring daylight escape from prison and his voluntary return and surrender later that evening. When reporters asked him why he had come back, he said, "The minute I sneaked home to see my wife, the first thing she said was, 'Where have you been? You escaped eight hours ago!'"

Hijack

About a month ago I was flying to Miami and a nervous little guy sitting next to me took out a gun and said, "Tell the pilot to take me to Rio de Janeiro."

I said, "You mean Havana."

He said, "Don't mix me up. This is my first hijack."

❧

Teacher: Where's your homework this morning?

Student: You'll never believe this, but on the way to school I made a paper airplane out of it and someone hijacked it to Cuba!

Hog Caller

A local pastor joined a community service club and the members thought they would have some fun with him. Under his name on the badge they printed "Hog Caller" as his occupation.

Everyone made a big fanfare as the badge was presented. The pastor responded by saying, "I usually am called 'Shepherd of the Sheep' . . . but you know your people better than I do."

Holy Matrimony

A minister forgot the name of a couple he was going to marry so he said from the pulpit, "Will those wishing to be united in holy matrimony please come forward after the service?"

After the service thirteen old maids came forward.

Horse Sense

Q: What is another name for stable thinking?

A: Horse sense.

HORSESHOE

A village blacksmith working at his open forge, hammering a white-hot horseshoe, had just finished the shoe and thrown it to the ground to cool.

The local wise-guy walked in at that moment. He picked up the horseshoe, but dropped it with a howl of pain.

"Pretty hot, eh?" asked the blacksmith.

"Naw," said the wise-guy. "It just don't take me long to look over a horseshoe."

HOTELS

Guest: What on earth do you put in your mattresses?
Innkeeper: The finest straw, Sir.
Guest: Now I know where the straw that broke the camel's back came from.

Scott: I went to a hotel for a change and rest.
Tim: Did you get it?
Scott: The bellboy got the change and the hotel got the rest.

HOURGLASS FIGURE

"Olive has the same hourglass figure she had when we were married, except now it could hold more sand."

HOUSEWIFE DEPRESSION

Three causes of housewife depression: ABC . . . NBC . . . CBS.

How's That?

"Our paper is two days late this week," wrote an Idaho newspaper editor, "owing to an accident. When we started to run the press Monday night, one of the guy ropes gave way, allowing the forward glider fluke to fall and break as it struck the flunker flopper. This, of course, as anyone who knows anything about a press will readily understand, left the gangplank with only the flip-flap to support it, which also dropped and broke off the wooper-cock. This loosened the fluking between the ramrod and the flibber-snatcher, which caused trouble with the mogus.

"The report that the delay was caused by our overindulgence in stimulants is a tissue of falsehoods. The redness in the appearance of our right eyes was caused by our going into the hatchway of the press in our anxiety to start it, and pulling the coppling pin after the slap-bang was broken, which caused the dingus to rise up and welt us in the optic. We expect a brand new glider fluke on this afternoon's train."

Hudson

A boastful Britisher was holding forth on the merits of his watch to friends in New York City. At last one of the Americans decided he could stand it no longer.

"That's nothing," he interrupted. "I dropped my watch into the Hudson a year ago, and it's been running ever since."

The Englishman looked taken aback.

"What?" he exclaimed. "The same watch?"

"No," he replied, "the Hudson."

Human Errors

The airline company was disturbed over a high percentage of accidents, and decided to eliminate human errors by building a completely mechanical plane.

"Ladies and gentlemen," came a voice over the loudspeaker on the maiden voyage, "it may interest you to know that you are now traveling in the world's first completely automatic plane. Now just sit back and relax because nothing can possibly go wrong . . . go wrong . . . go wrong . . . go wrong."

Hunter

A sportsman went to a hunting lodge and bagged a record number of birds, aided by a dog named Salesman. Next year he returned and asked for Salesman again. "The hound ain't no durn good now," the handler said.

"What happened!" cried the sportsman. "Was he injured?"

"No. Some fool came down here and called him 'Sales Manager' all week instead of Salesman. Now all he does is sit on his tail and bark."

∽

Little John: I used to be a big-game hunter. Why, for years I shot elephants in Alaska.

Big Alfred: That's impossible! There aren't any elephants in Alaska.

Little John: Of course not. I shot them all.

Husbands and Wives

"Did you hear about the guy that had three wives in three months? The first two died of poisoned mushrooms."

"What happened to the third wife?"

"She died from a blow on the head. She wouldn't eat the mushrooms!"

∽

Husband: One more payment and the furniture is ours.

Wife: Oh, good. Then we can throw it out and get some new stuff.

∽

My husband really embarrassed me the other day in a restaurant. When he drank his soup, six couples got up and started to dance.

ᓚ

Wife: When we were younger, you used to nibble on my ear.
Husband: Excuse me. I'll be right back.
Wife: Where are you going?
Husband: I'm going to get my teeth.

ᓚ

"What did your husband get you for your birthday?"
"A smog device."
"Why a smog device?"
"He said my breath was a major cause of air pollution."

ᓚ

"I wonder if my husband will love me when my hair is gray."
"Why not? He's loved you through three shades already."

ᓚ

There are only two ways to handle a woman and nobody knows either of them.

ᓚ

"Now, that looks like a happily married couple."
"Don't be too sure, My Dear. They're probably saying the same thing about us."

ᓚ

She: I had to marry you to find out how stupid you are.
He: You should have known that the minute I asked you.

ᓚ

The cooing usually stops when the honeymoon is over, but the billing goes on forever.

∽

"Did your wife have much to say when you got home last night?"
"No, but that didn't keep her from talking for two hours."

∽

Wife: I just got back from the beauty shop.
Husband: What was the matter? Was it closed?

∽

Wife: I dreamed you gave me $100 for summer clothes last night. You wouldn't spoil that dream, would you, Dear?
Husband: Of course not, Darling. You may keep the $100.

∽

Wife: You both arrived at that cab at the same time. Why did you let him have it? Why didn't you stand up for your rights?
Husband: He needed it more than I did. He was late to his karate class.

∽

Wife I: Does your husband have ulcers?
Wife II: No, but he's a carrier!

∽

A man entered a bank with a gun in his hand. He bellowed, "I'm going to rob every man in this bank, and I'm going to kiss every woman."
One of the men who had accompanied his wife to the bank said, "You may rob all of us men, but you're not going to kiss all the ladies!"

His wife punched him in the ribs and said, "Now leave him alone, George. He's robbing the bank."

☙

The best way for a man to remember his wife's birthday is to forget it just once.

HUSBANDS

"My husband just ran off with someone else. I can hardly control myself."
"Go ahead and let go, Dearie. You'll feel better after a good laugh."

☙

Betty: Does your husband ever take advice?
Sue: Occasionally, when nobody is looking.

☙

Sally: I wonder what's wrong with that tall blond guy over there. Just a minute ago he was getting awful friendly, and then all of a sudden he turned pale, walked away, and won't even look at me anymore.
Linda: Maybe he saw me come in. He's my husband.

❧ I ❧

I Remember

Father: When I was your age, I was up at five every morning. I fed the chickens, cleared the snow from around the house, and then did my six-mile paper route. And I thought nothing of it.

Son: I don't blame you, Dad. I don't think much of it, either.

Ideal Preacher

He preaches exactly twenty minutes and then sits down. He condemns sin, but never hurts anyone's feelings. He works from 8:00 A.M. to 10:00 P.M. in every type of work, from preaching to taxi service. He makes sixty dollars a week, wears good clothes, buys good books regularly, has a nice family, drives a good car, and gives thirty dollars a week to the church. He also stands ready to contribute to every good work that comes along. He is twenty-six years old and has been preaching for thirty years. He is tall and short, thin and heavyset, plain-looking but handsome. He has one brown eye and one blue, hair parted in the middle, left side straight and dark, the other side wavy and blond. He has a burning desire to work with teenagers, and spends all his time with the older folks. He smiles all the time with a straight face because he has a sense of humor that keeps him seriously dedicated to his work.

He makes fifteen calls a day on church members, spends all his time evangelizing the unchurched, and is never out of his office. He is truly a remarkable person . . . and he does not exist.

Idiot

"When I was a child I used to bite my fingernails, and the doctor told me if I didn't quit I'd grow up to be an idiot."

"And you couldn't stop, huh?"

∽

Do you know how to keep an idiot in suspense? I'll tell you tomorrow.

I'm Fine

I'm fine, I'm fine.
There's nothing whatever the matter with me,
I'm just as healthy as I can be.
I have arthritis in both of my knees
And when I talk, I talk with a wheeze.
My pulse is weak and my blood is thin
But I'm awfully well for the shape I'm in.
My teeth eventually will have to come out
And I can't hear a word unless you shout.
I'm overweight and I can't get thin
But I'm awfully well for the shape I'm in.
Arch supports I have for my feet
Or I wouldn't be able to walk down the street.
Sleep is denied me every night
And every morning I'm really a sight.
My memory is bad and my head's a-spin
And I practically live on aspirin.
But I'm awfully well for the shape I'm in.
The moral is, as this tale unfolds,
That for you and me who are growing old,
It's better to say, "I'm fine," with a grin
Than to let people know the shape we're in!

Improve

Of all the awkward people in your house, there is only one you can improve very much.

Indians

Did you hear about the Indian chief named Running Water? He had two daughters—Hot and Cold—and a son named Luke.

ᴄᴏ

An Indian from a reservation in Arizona was visiting Washington, D.C. While wandering around the town, he was stopped by a native of the city who asked, "How do you like our town?"

"All right," said the Indian. "And how do you like our country?"

In-Laws

Rob: Why do you have your front door leading right into your dining room?

Jim: So my wife's relatives won't have to waste any time.

∽

"My mother-in-law passed away last week."

"What was the complaint?"

"There was no complaint. Everybody was satisfied."

Innocent

Policeman: Here is your parking ticket.

Woman: And just what do you do when you catch a real criminal?

Policeman: I don't know . . . all I ever catch are the innocent ones.

Insects

"This is an ideal spot for a picnic."

"It must be. Fifty-million insects can't be wrong."

Insomnia

As they were leaving church one Sunday, a man confided to his friend that he was suffering from insomnia. The friend asserted that he had no trouble getting to sleep.

"Really?" the first man inquired. "Do you count sheep?"

"No," was the retort. "I talk to the shepherd."

∽

"Do you know of any cures for insomnia?"
"Try talking to yourself."

Insurance

The following quotations were taken from a Toronto newspaper. They are samples of comments that individuals wrote down on their claim forms following their auto accidents:

I misjudged a lady crossing the street.

Coming home, I drove into the wrong house and collided with a tree I don't have.

I collided with a stationary streetcar coming from the opposite direction.

The other car collided with mine without giving warning of its intentions.

I heard a horn blow and was struck in the back—a lady was evidently trying to pass me.

I thought my window was down, but found it was up when I put my hand through it.

My car was stolen, and I sent up a human cry but it has not been recovered.

The truck backed through my windshield into my wife's face.

A pedestrian hit me and went under my car.

The guy was all over the road. I had to swerve a number of times before I hit him.

If the other driver had stopped a few yards behind himself, the accident would not have happened.

In my attempt to kill a fly, I drove into a telephone pole.

I had been shopping for plants all day, and was on my way home. As I reached an intersection, a hedge sprang up, obscuring my vision. I did not see the other car.

I had been driving my car for forty years when I fell asleep at the wheel and had an accident.

I was on my way to the doctor's with rear-end trouble when my universal joint gave way, causing me to have an accident.

My car was legally parked as it backed into the other vehicle.

An invisible car came out of nowhere, struck my vehicle, and vanished.

I told the police that I was not injured, but on removing my hat, I found that I had a skull fracture.

I was sure the old fellow would never make it to the other side of the roadway when I struck him.

The pedestrian had no idea which way to go, so I ran over him.

The indirect cause of this accident was a little guy in a small car with a big mouth.

I was thrown from my car as it left the road. I was later found in a ditch by some stray cows.

The telephone pole was approaching fast. I was attempting to swerve out of its path when it struck my front end.

I was unable to stop in time, and my car crashed into the other vehicle. The driver and passengers then left immediately for a vacation with injuries.

I pulled away from the side of the road, glanced at my mother-in-law, and headed over the embankment.

∽

Jack: Don't you know that you can't sell insurance without a license?
Buck: I knew I wasn't selling any, but I didn't know the reason.

INTRODUCTION

Our speaker for the evening gives the most refreshing talks. Everywhere he goes the audiences always feel good when they wake up.

∽

A Londoner wound up a business trip to the Orient with a visit to Taipei. At a luncheon he was asked to say a few words. Since he spoke not a word of Chinese, his address was to be translated by an interpreter sentence by sentence.

"Well," he began, "I just want you to know that I'm tickled to death to be here."

A look of agony appeared on the interpreter's face. "This poor man," he said in halting Chinese, "scratches himself until he dies, only to be with you."

∽

Recently our speaker had to discontinue several of his long talks on account of his throat. Several people threatened to cut it.

∾

Tonight I would like to present to you _____ of whom the President of the United States once said: "Who?"

∾

Our speaker will not bore you with a long speech—he can do it with a short one.

∾

It is said that _____ is the greatest speaker in the business. And tonight we honor the man who made that statement, _____.

∾

After a very long introduction, the evening speaker got up and said, "Now I know how a pancake feels when they pour syrup on it."

∾

I'm sorry to announce we have two disappointments tonight. Robert Redford couldn't make it, and _____ could.

∾

You've been a wonderful audience—you stayed.

∾

As master of ceremonies, I am not going to stand up here and tell you a lot of old jokes. Our speaker, Mr. _____, will do that for me.

∾

Our speaker needs no introduction. What he needs is a conclusion.

INVENTOR

The most famous Irish inventor was Pat Pending.

∽

Did you hear about the new invention? A square bathtub! It eliminates the ring!

IRS

A businessman who was near death asked that his remains be cremated and the ashes be mailed to the Internal Revenue Service with the following note attached: "Now You Have It All."

∽

April is always a difficult month for Americans. Even if your ship comes in, the IRS is right there to help you unload it.

∽

If your face is your fortune, you won't have to pay any income tax.

∽

Did you hear about the man from the income tax bureau who phoned a certain Baptist minister to say, "We're checking the tax return of a member of your church, Deacon X, and notice he lists a donation to your building fund of three hundred dollars. Is that correct?"

The minister answered without hesitation, "I haven't got my records available, but I'll promise you one thing: If he hasn't, he will!"

ISAIAH

Q: Do you know what the name of Isaiah's horse was?
A: Is Me. He said, "Woe, is me."

It's All in the Family

Talk about children mimicking their parents! I understand Hollywood kids don't play doctor and nurse anymore. It's psychiatrist and psychoneurotic!

☙

The average man's life consists of twenty years of having his mother ask him where he is going; forty years of having his wife ask the same question; and at the end, the mourners wonder, too.

☙

The cheapest way to have your family tree traced is to run for a public office.

☙

A man I know solved the problem of too many visiting relatives. He borrowed money from the rich ones and loaned it to the poor ones. Now none of them come back.

☙

Real estate salesman: Could I interest you in a home?
Man: What do I need a home for? I was born in a hospital, educated in a college, courted in an automobile, and married in a church. I live out of tin cans, cellophane bags, and delicatessen stores. I spend my mornings at the office, the afternoons on the golf course, and my evenings at the movies. When I die, I'm going to be buried in the ground. I don't need a home, all I need is a garage.

☙

If you want to avoid domestic strife, don't marry in January . . . and that goes for the other months, too.

☙

Husband: Now look, Lucy. I don't want to seem harsh, but your mother has been living with us for twenty years now. Don't you think it's about time she got a place of her own?

Wife: *My* mother? I thought she was *your* mother!

∽

Before I got married, I had six theories about bringing up children. Now I have six children and no theories.

∽

"In our family," a little girl told her teacher, "everybody marries relatives. My father married my mother, my uncle married my aunt, and the other day I found that my grandmother married my grandfather."

∽

Views expressed by husbands are not necessarily those of the management.

❧ J ❧

JEWELS

A woman making arrangements with an artist to sit for her portrait said to him, "Although I have only a few items of jewelry, I want this painting to show me wearing diamond rings and earrings, an emerald brooch, and a multistrand necklace of pearls that look like they are priceless."

"I can do this all right," said the artist. "But do you mind telling me why you want this, when apparently you do not particularly care for jewelry?"

"You see, if I die first," said the woman, "and my husband marries again, I want that second wife to go out of her mind trying to find out where he hid the jewels."

JOAN OF ARC

A little boy, just back from Sunday school, asked his father if Noah had a wife.

"All the time, questions, questions, questions," replied the father. "Of course he did: Joan of Arc."

JOKES

"When I tell jokes people clap their hands."
"Yeah, clap them over their ears."

∽

Q: How do you make an Englishman happy in his old age?
A: Tell him jokes when he is still young.

∽

Diplomat: One who never heard that old joke before.

JUDGMENT

Husband: You must admit that men have better judgment than women.
Wife: Oh, yes. You married me, and I married you.

JURY

Mrs. Franklin had been called for jury duty. She declined to serve because, she said, she did not believe in capital punishment. The judge tried to persuade her to stay. "Madam," he said, "this is not a murder case. It is merely a case in which a wife is suing her husband because she gave him $4,000 to buy her a new fur coat and he lost it all at the racetrack instead."

"I'll serve," agreed Mrs. Franklin. "I could be wrong about capital punishment."

⋇ K ⋇

Kibitzer

All evening long, four card players had been pestered by a kibitzer. When he went out of the room for a moment, they hit on a plan to silence him. "Let's make up a game no one ever heard of," one of them said. "Then he'll have to shut up."

The kibitzer returned. The dealer tore two cards in half and gave them to the man on his left. He tore the corners off three cards and spread them out in front of the man opposite him. Then he tore five cards in quarters, gave 15 pieces to the man on his right and kept five himself. "I have a mingle," he said. "I'll bet a dollar."

"I have a snazzle," the next man announced. "I'll raise you a dollar."

The third man folded without betting.

The fourth, after due deliberation, said, "I've got a farfle. I'll raise you two dollars."

The kibitzer shook his head vehemently. "You're crazy," he said. "You're never going to beat a mingle and a snazzle with a lousy farfle!"

Kids

A little boy never said a word for six years. One day his parents served him cocoa. From out of left field the kid said, "This cocoa's no good."

His parents went around raving. They asked him, "Why did you wait so long to talk?"

He said, "Up till now everything's been okay."

∽

Father: Do you think it will improve Junior's behavior if we buy him a bicycle?

Mother: No, but it'll spread his behavior over a wider area.

∽

131

Dad: How dare you kick your little brother in the stomach!
Son: It's his own fault, Daddy. He turned around.

∽

An exasperated mother, whose son was always getting into mischief, finally asked him, "How do you expect to get into heaven?"
The boy thought it over and said, "Well, I'll just run in and out and in and out and keep slamming the door until St. Peter says, 'For heaven's sake, Jimmy, come in or stay out.'"

∽

"Billy, get your little brother's hat out of that mud puddle."
"I can't, Ma. He's got it strapped too tight under his chin."

∽

Billy was in a store with his mother when he was given a stick of candy by one of the clerks.
"What do you say, Billy?" said his mother.
"Charge it," he replied.

∽

"Mother, do give me another piece of sugar," said little Helen.
"But you've had three already," her mother pointed out.
"Just one more, please."
"Well, this must be the last."
"Thank you, Mother . . . but I must say, you have no will power."

∽

Today we spend $60,000 for a school bus to pick up the kids right at the door so they don't have to walk. Then we spend over a million dollars for a gym so the kids can get some exercise.

∽

These children are nuts today. I have a child myself, ten years old. He's going to be eleven . . . if I let him!

∽

Lady: Oh, isn't he sweet. . . . Little boy, if you give me a kiss, I'll give you a bright new penny.

Little boy: I get twice as much at home for just taking castor oil.

∽

Mother: Your face is clean, but how did you get your hands so dirty?

Son: Washin' my face.

∽

The mother said firmly, "If you two boys can't agree and be quiet, I shall take your pie away."

The younger one replied, "But, Mother, we do agree; Bill wants the biggest piece, and so do I!"

∽

Jed: Your sister is spoiled, isn't she?

Ted: No, that's the perfume she uses.

∽

There was an earthquake recently which frightened inhabitants of a certain town. One couple sent their little boy to stay with an uncle in another district, explaining the reason for the nephew's sudden visit. A day later the parents received this telegram: "Am returning your boy. Send the earthquake."

∽

Mother: Eat your spinach. It will put color in your cheeks.

Son: Who wants green cheeks?

∽

Mother: Why did you fall in the mud puddle with your new dress on?
Sally: There wasn't time to take it off.

❦

The trouble with your children is that when they're not being a lump in your throat, they're being a pain in your neck.

KING OF SIAM

Rich: I once sang for the king of Siam. At least that's what he told me he was.
Dave: Yes. He said, "If you're a singer, then I'm the king of Siam."

KING OF THE WORLD

Husband: I know you are having a lot of trouble with the baby, dear, but keep in mind: "The hand that rocks the cradle is the hand that rules the world."
Wife: How about taking over the world for a few hours while I go shopping?

KIPPER

For many years a certain white whale and a tiny herring had been inseparable friends. Wherever the white whale roamed in search of food, the herring was sure to be swimming right along beside him.
One fine spring day the herring turned up off the coast of Norway without his companion. Naturally all the other fish were curious, and an octopus finally asked the herring what happened to his whale friend.
"How should I know?" the herring replied. "Am I my blubber's kipper?"

KISS

Father: When I was your age, I never kissed a girl. Will you be able to tell your children that?
Son: Not with a straight face.

❦

Stealing a kiss may be petty larceny, but sometimes it's grand.

Kiss a Mule

A little prospector wearing clean new shoes walked into a saloon. A big Texan said to his friend standing at the bar, "Watch me make this dude dance." He walked over to the prospector and said, "You're a foreigner, aren't you? From the East?"

"You might say that," the little prospector answered. "I'm from Boston and I'm here prospecting for gold."

"Now tell me something. Can you dance?"

"No, sir. I never did learn to dance."

"Well, I'm going to teach you. You'll be surprised how quickly you can learn."

With that, the Texan took out his gun and started shooting at the prospector's feet. Hopping, skipping, jumping—by the time the little prospector made it to the door he was shaking like a leaf.

About an hour later the Texan left the saloon. As soon as he stepped outside the door, he heard a click. He looked around and there, four feet from his head, was the biggest shotgun he had ever seen.

And the little prospector said, "Mr. Texan, have you ever kissed a mule?"

"No," said the quick-thinking Texan, "but I've always wanted to."

Knock, Knock

"Knock, knock."
"Who's there?"
"Mayonnaise."
"Mayonnaise who?"
"Mayonnaise have seen the glory of. . . ."

∞

"Knock, knock."
"Who's there?"
"Della."
"Della who?"
"Della Katessen."

∞

"Knock, knock."
"Who's there?"
"Amos."
"Amos who?"
"A mosquito bit me."
"Knock, knock."
"Who's there?"
"Andy."
"Andy who?"
"And he bit me again."

∽

"Knock, knock."
"Who's there?"
"Banana."
"Banana who?"
"Knock, knock."
"Who's there?"
"Banana."
"Banana who?"
"Knock, knock."
"Who's there?"
"Orange."
"Orange who?"
"Orange you glad I didn't say 'banana' again?"

∽

"Knock, knock."
"Who's there?"
"Gorilla."
"Gorilla who?"
"Gorilla my dreams, I love you."

⁂ L ⁂

Landlord

"Twenty years from now," said a poor writer who was having trouble with his landlord, "people will come by and look at this house and say, 'Phillips, the famous writer, had a room here.'"

The landlord was unimpressed. "Phillips, I'm telling you that if you don't pay your rent, they'll be saying that the day after tomorrow!"

The Last Lapp

If you're traveling in Scandinavia and you come to the last Lapp, you must be near the Finnish line.

Last Words

"Have you any last words," the warden asked the condemned man, "before we hang you?"

"Yes," panted the prisoner, "just get it over with quickly, please!"

The warden patted the man on the back, gave the signal, and the condemned man was dropped through the platform. But he didn't die. He kept bouncing up and down. So they drew him up and dropped him again. But still he didn't die; he just bounced up and down. Spectators began to faint as they heard the prisoner gasp, "C'mon and get through with this!"

So they lifted him up again and dropped him again, and once more he bobbed up and down at the end of the rope. The executioner was in a cold sweat and the guards had all they could do to keep the warden from passing out. When they drew him up for the eleventh time, the prisoner, eyeballs popping and tongue lolling out the side of his mouth, demanded, "C'mon and get through with this! What am I—a murderer or a yo-yo?"

LAW

A newspaper columnist was found guilty and fined for calling a countess a cow. When the trial ended and the man paid his fine, he asked the judge if, since it was now clear he could not call a countess a cow, he could call a cow a countess.

The judge said that was all right to do. Whereupon the newspaperman turned toward the countess in the courtroom, bowed elaborately, and said, "How do you do, Countess."

∽

A modern murderer is supposed to be innocent until he is proven insane.

LAWYER

Lawyer: Seventy-five dollars, please.
Client: What for?
Lawyer: My advice.
Client: I'm not taking it.

∽

Lawyer: Now repeat to the court, word-for-word, what the defendant said.
Witness: I'd rather not. They're not words fit to tell a gentleman.
Lawyer: In that case, lean over and whisper them in my ear.

∽

John: Why don't you go to a lawyer with your problem?
Glen: My brother said any fool could advise me, so I came to you.

∽

My son, a lawyer, was approached by his friend, a priest, who wanted a will drawn up. When the work was completed and ready to be mailed, my son couldn't resist inserting this note: "Thy Will Be Done."

∽

First boy: A little bird told me what kind of lawyer your father is.
Second boy: What did he say?
First boy: Cheep! Cheep!
Second boy: Oh, yeah. Well, a duck just told me what kind of doctor your father is.

∽

A famous trial lawyer was asked to apologize to the court for some remarks he had made. With dignity, he bowed to the judge and said: "Your Honor is right, and I am wrong, as Your Honor generally is."

The judge never figured out whether he should be satisfied with this remark or cite the lawyer for contempt of court.

∽

An old miser, because of his exceptional thrift, had no friends. Just before he died he called his doctor, lawyer, and minister together around his bedside. "I have always heard you can't take it with you, but I am going to prove you can," he said. "I have $90,000 in cash under my mattress. It's in three envelopes of $30,000 each. I want each of you to take one envelope now and just before they throw the dirt on me, you throw the envelopes in."

The three attended the funeral, and each threw his envelope into the grave. On the way back from the cemetery, the minister said, "I don't feel exactly right. I'm going to confess: I needed $10,000 badly for a new church we are building, so I took out $10,000 and threw only $20,000 in the grave."

The doctor said, "I, too, must confess: I am building a hospital and took $20,000 and threw in only $10,000."

The lawyer said, "Gentlemen, I'm surprised, shocked, and ashamed of you. I don't see how you could hold out that money. I threw in my personal check for the full amount."

჻

A lawyer is a man who gets two other men to strip for a fight and then takes their clothes.

჻

"I'm looking for a criminal lawyer. Have you one here?"
"Well, we think we have, but we can't prove it yet."

჻

Lawyer: Are you positive that the prisoner is the man who stole your car?
Witness: Well, I was until you cross-examined me. Now I'm not sure whether I ever had a car at all.

჻

"What is wrong when you have a lawyer buried up to his neck in the sand?"
"You don't have enough sand."

჻

A burglar's wife was being cross-examined by the district attorney.
Attorney: Are you the wife of this prisoner?
Woman: Yes.
Attorney: You knew he was a burglar when you married him?
Woman: Yes.
Attorney: May I ask how you came to marry such an individual?
Woman: You may. You see, I was getting older and had to choose between marrying a burglar or a lawyer.

LAZY

"He is the idol of the family."
"Yes, he has been idle for twenty years."

∽

"You're the laziest man I ever saw. Don't you do anything quickly?"
"Yes, I get tired fast."

LEFTOVERS

A preacher forgot his notes for the sermon he was going to deliver. In the midst of the sermon he got a few things twisted when he said that the Lord took four thousand barley loaves and six thousand fishes and fed twenty-four people, and had plenty left over.

Someone in the congregation called out, "Anybody could do that."

"Could you?" asked the minister.

"Certainly I could."

After the service, when the minister complained about the heckler's conduct, he was told of his error by a deacon. "Well, next week I will not forget my notes. I'll fix that character."

The next week the minister stepped forward confidently and began his sermon. In the course of it, he brought up again the miracle of the loaves and fishes. He told how the five barley loaves and the two fishes had fed the multitude of probably twenty-four thousand people. He then pointed to the heckler from the previous Sunday and asked, "Could you do that?"

"I sure could," said the heckler.

"And just how would you do that?" asked the minister.

"With the loaves and fishes left over from last Sunday."

LETTER

Suddenly called out of town, a news commentator told his new secretary: "Write Allis-Chalmers in Milwaukee. Say that I can't keep that appointment Friday. I'm off for Texas. I'll telephone when I get back. Sign my name."

Upon his return, he found this carbon waiting:
Alice Chalmers
Milwaukee, Wisconsin
Dear Alice:
I'm off for Texas and can't keep that date . . .
The man promptly phoned the tractor company and said, "I hope you haven't received a certain letter."
"Received it!" came the reply. "It's been on the bulletin board for three days!"

LIAR

Joe: Is that all there is to the story?
Joan: I guess so. I've already told you more than I heard.

⌒

"I'm not a liar, sir. I just remember big!"

LICENSE

Two fellows out hunting were stopped by a game warden. One of them took off running and the game warden went after him and caught him. The fellow then showed the warden his hunting license.
"Why did you run when you had a license?"
"Because the other fellow didn't have one."

LIE

A minister spoke to a deacon and said, "I'm told you went to the ball game instead of church this morning." "That's a lie," said the deacon, "and here's the fish to prove it."

LIE DETECTOR

First man: Have you ever seen one of those machines that can tell when a person is telling a lie?
Second man: Seen one? I married one!

LIGHTWEIGHTS

First woman: How do you like my new dress?
Second woman: Fine—but you didn't take the hanger out.
First woman: Those are my shoulder blades.

❧

He's so thin his muscles look like flea bites on a piece of spaghetti.

❧

The world's skinniest kid is the girl who was so thin that if she stood sideways, she was marked absent. If she took a nickel out of her pocket, it threw her off balance.

❧

She recently swallowed an olive and was rushed to a maternity hospital.

❧

She is so thin it takes two of her to make a shadow.

LITTLE LIONS

A small man said to a large man, "If I were as big as you, I would go into the jungle, find me a big lion, and pull him limb from limb."
The big man replied, "There are some little lions in the jungle, too. Let's see what you can do."

LOAN

Max: You couldn't loan me twenty dollars, could you?
Jeff: No, but how did you know it?

❧

A rather frugal man asked the bank for a loan of one dollar and was told he would have to pay seven percent interest at the end of the year. For security he offered $60,000 in U.S. bonds. The banker, foreseeing a potential depositor, accepted the bonds and gave the man a dollar.

At the end of the year, he was back with a dollar and seven cents to clear up his debt and asked for the return of his bonds. Upon returning the bonds the banker asked, "I don't want to be inquisitive, but since you have all those bonds, why did you have to borrow a dollar?"

"Well," said the tightfisted old gent, "I really didn't have to. But do you know of any other way I could get the use of a safety deposit box for seven cents a year?

∽

John: Lend me fifty.
Jack: I have only forty.
John: Well, then let me have the forty and you can owe me the ten.

∽

"I think you're a nice kid. I've known you for about five years. Could you let me have five dollars?"

"I'm sorry—I couldn't."

"Why?"

"Because I have known you for five years."

∽

Whenever my wife needs money, she calls me handsome. She says, "Hand some over."

∽

Wife: I'm happy to see that the neighbors finally returned our lawn mower before they moved. They certainly had it long enough.

Husband: Our lawn mower? I just bought it at the garage sale they're having.

∽

Myles: Suppose you loan Ralph ten dollars and he agrees to repay you at the rate of a dollar a week. How much money would you have after seven weeks?

Jay: Nothing.

Myles: Nothing? You don't know very much about math.

Jay: You don't know much about Ralph.

∽

"I'm looking for somebody to lend me fifty dollars."

"Well, you certainly have a nice day for it."

Long Evening

After a long evening of conversation the host said, "I hate to put you out, but I have to get up at six o'clock in the morning to catch a plane."

"Good heavens," said the guest. "I thought you were at my house!"

Lost and Found

Bill: I just found this nice new penknife on the sidewalk.

Dad: Are you sure it was lost?

Bill: I'm very sure. I saw the man looking for it.

Lot's Wife

The Sunday school teacher was describing how Lot's wife looked back and suddenly turned into a pillar of salt.

"My mother looked back once while she was driving," contributed little Johnny, "and she turned into a telephone pole."

Love

Love may not make the world spin around, but it certainly makes a lot of people dizzy.

∽

Here's to love—the only fire for which there is no insurance.

∽

A kiss is a peculiar proposition—of no use to one, yet absolute bliss to two. The small boy gets it for nothing, the young man has to lie for it, and the old man has to buy it. It is the baby's right, the lover's privilege, and the hypocrite's mask. To a young girl, it shows faith; to a married woman, hope; and to an old maid, charity.

∽

Linda: Do you really love me, or do you just think you do?
Jack: Honey, I really love you. I haven't done any thinking yet.

∽

Girl: Do you love me?
Boy: Yes, Dear.
Girl: Would you die for me?
Boy: No—mine is an undying love.

∽

He: I love you terribly.
She: You certainly do.

∽

Love may be blind, but it seems to be able to find its way around in the dark.

∽

Love is said to be blind, but I know lots of fellows who can see twice as much in their sweethearts as I can.

∽

Love is sometimes like a poisoned mushroom. You can't tell if it's the real thing until it's too late.

Luck

I believe in luck. How else can you explain the success of those you dislike?

—Jean Cocteau

∽

Depend on the rabbit's foot if you will, but remember it didn't work for the rabbit.

—R.E. Shay

❧ M ❧

MAHARAJA

The maharaja of an Indian province decreed a ban on hunting wildlife, and soon the country was overrun with man-eating animals. When the people could stand it no longer, they gave the maharaja the heave-ho. This may be the first time in history when the reign was called on account of game.

MANSLAUGHTER

A man charged with murder bribed a friend on the jury to hold out for a verdict of manslaughter. The jury was out for a long period of time, but at last brought in a verdict of manslaughter.

Upon visiting the prisoner the following week, the friend was thanked. "You must have had a tough time getting them to vote for manslaughter."

"Tough is right," replied the friend. "The other eleven wanted to acquit you."

MARILYN MONROE

Wife: And Francois, the great expert on beautiful women, told me that I can match my legs with Marilyn Monroe's.

Husband: How can you match your legs with Monroe's? They don't even match each other!

MARK TWAIN

"Reader, suppose you were an idiot. And suppose you were a member of Congress. But I repeat myself."

—*Mark Twain*

Mark Twain said that when he was young he was impressed by the story of a young man who landed a job when the employer saw him pick up several pins from the sidewalk outside the firm's office.

So Twain went to the street alongside the office windows of a firm he wanted to work for and began almost ostentatiously to pick up pins he had earlier placed on the sidewalk. After a good number of pins had been picked up, a clerk came out and said, "The boss asked me to tell you to move along. Your idiotic behavior is distracting the people working in the office."

MARRIAGE

Wife: I should have listened to my mother's advice and never married you.
Husband: Good grief! How I've misjudged that woman.

ᦕ

Attendant: Doctor, there is a man outside who wants to know if we've lost any of our men from the insane asylum.
Doctor: Why's that?
Attendant: He says that someone has run off with his wife.

ᦕ

My wife told the neighbors that thirty years ago she had a close encounter with a subhuman alien creature from outer space, but never reported it to the authorities. Instead, she married it.

ᦕ

"Time separates the best of friends."
"So does money."
"And don't forget marriage."

ᦕ

Sue: See that woman over there? She's been married four times—once to a millionaire, then to an actor, then to a minister, and last to an undertaker.

Sal: I know! One for the money, two for the show, three to get ready, and four to go!

~

Nancy: What excuse have you for not being married?
Rich: I was born that way.

~

"How long have you two been married?" asked a friend.
"We've been happily married for seven years," answered the husband. "Seven out of sixteen isn't bad."

~

The honeymoon is over when he no longer smiles gently as he scrapes the burnt toast.

~

A wife is the only person who can look into the top drawer of a dresser and find a man's socks that aren't there.

~

Despite the statistics, he denies that married men live longer than single men . . . it only seems longer.

~

Son: Do you think a man has more sense after he is married?
Father: Yes, but it's too late then.

~

Boy: Do you know, Dad, that in some parts of Africa a man doesn't know his wife until he marries her?
Dad: Why single out Africa?

~

You can always tell when a marriage is shaky. The partners don't even talk to each other during a television commercial.

ᔕᕽ

Marriage is nature's way of keeping people from fighting with strangers.

ᔕᕽ

Women are fools to marry men. On the other hand, what else is there to marry?

ᔕᕽ

Son: Dad, does bigamy mean that a man has one wife too many?
Dad: Not necessarily, Son. A man can have one wife too many and still not be a bigamist.

ᔕᕽ

Being a husband is like any other job. It helps a lot if you like the boss.

ᔕᕽ

"If you refuse to marry me, I will die," said the young romantic. And, sure enough, fifty years later he died.

ᔕᕽ

It is very warm and reassuring to know that when you get married, no matter what comes along, you'll always have somebody at your side to blame it on.

ᔕᕽ

Before marriage a man declares that he will be the boss in his home or know the reason why; after marriage he knows the reason why.

ᔕᕽ

A couple was celebrating their golden wedding anniversary. Their domestic tranquillity had long been the talk of the town. A local newspaper reporter was inquiring as to the secret of their long and happy marriage.

"Well, it dates back to our honeymoon," explained the lady. "We visited the Grand Canyon and took a trip down to the bottom of the canyon by pack mule. We hadn't gone too far when my husband's mule stumbled. My husband took the mule by the ears, shook him vigorously and said, 'That's once.' We proceeded a little farther when the mule stumbled again. Once more my husband took him by the ears, shook him even more vigorously and said, 'That's twice.' We hadn't gone a half-mile when the mule stumbled a third time. My husband promptly removed a revolver from his pocket and shot him. I started to protest over his treatment of the mule when he grabbed me by the ears, shook me vigorously, and said, 'That's once.'"

∽

It has been proven that married life is healthy. Statistics show that single people die sooner than married folks. So, if you're looking for a long life and a slow death, get married!

∽

A man who traveled to Iran was telling a large audience about how careless the men over there are with their wives. He said it was not an uncommon sight to see a woman and a donkey hitched up together.

From the back of his audience a woman's voice was heard to say, "That's not so unusual. You often see it over here, too."

∽

Marriage is like a midnight phone call—you get a ring, and then you wake up.

∽

A man is incomplete until he's married . . . then he's finished.

∽

Buck: Were you ever married?
Glen: Yeah, but my wife ran away.
Buck: How did it happen?
Glen: She ran away when I was taking a bath.
Buck: I'll bet she waited years for the opportunity.

∞

Ben: I think she married me for my money.
Len: Well, she earned it.

∞

Before marriage a man thinks nothing is good enough for his wife. After marriage he still thinks nothing is good enough for her.

∞

Boy: Dad, I just got a part in the school play. I play the part of a man who's been married for twenty-five years.
Father: That's a good start, son. Just keep right at it and one of these days you'll get a speaking part!

Marriage Counselor

Marriage counselor to female client: Maybe your problem is that you've been waking up grumpy in the morning.
Client: No, I always let him sleep.

∞

A man who had been married for ten years was consulting a marriage counselor. "When I was first married, I was very happy. I'd come home from a hard day down at the shop, and my little dog would race around barking, and my wife would bring my slippers. Now everything's changed. When I come home, my dog brings my slippers, and my wife barks at me."

"I don't know what you're complaining about," said the counselor. "You're still getting the same service."

MARTIAN

A Martian wandered from his spaceship in the desert into Las Vegas and arrived when one of the slot machines was spewing forth a bunch of nickels. When the exploding gadget had subsided, the Martian went over to it and said, "With a cold like that, you ought to take some aspirin and get into bed."

MATHEMATICS

A Missouri farmer passed away and left 17 mules to his three sons. The instructions left in the will said that the oldest boy was to get one-half, the second eldest one-third, and the youngest one-ninth. The three sons, recognizing the difficulty of dividing 17 mules in these fractions, began to argue.

The uncle heard about the argument, hitched up his mule, and rode out to settle the matter. He added his mule to the 17, making 18. The eldest son therefore got one-half or nine; the second got one-third or six; and the youngest got one-ninth or two. Adding up 9, 6 and 2 equals 17. The uncle, having settled the argument, hitched up his mule and rode home.

MEDICALLY EXEMPT

A draftee went in for his physical wearing a truss and with papers that were stamped "M.E." for Medically Exempt.

Afterward a friend borrowed the truss to wear for his physical.

At the end of the examination the doctor stamped "M.E." on his papers. "Does that mean I'm Medically Exempt?" he asked the doctor.

"No," replied the doctor. "M.E. stands for Middle East. Anyone who can wear a truss upside down can ride a camel."

MEDICINE

Mother: Doctor, doctor! My little Billy swallowed a dozen aspirin. What should I do?

Doctor: Are you sure it was a dozen?

Mother: Absolutely! Doctor, I'm scared to death.

Doctor: Calm down. Is little Billy crying?
Mother: No.
Doctor: Is he sleeping?
Mother: No.
Doctor: Is his color funny?
Mother: No.
Doctor: Did he throw up?
Mother: No. But I'm scared. All that aspirin—shouldn't I do something?
Doctor: Try and give him a headache.

∽

"What are you taking for your cold?"
"I don't know. What will you give me?"

Mellow

A church soloist was delighted when one of the members spoke to him after church and said, "You have a very mellow voice."

The soloist went home and looked up the definition of the word "mellow" in his dictionary. He read: "Mellow: overripe and almost rotten."

Membership Drive

We had a membership drive in our church. Last week we drove off thirty-five.

Membrane

The part of your brain you remember with.

Memory

A tourist was introduced to an Indian in New Mexico who was said to have a perfect memory. Skeptical, the tourist asked, "What did you have for breakfast on September 10, 1943?"

The Indian answered, "Eggs."

The man scoffed, "Everyone eats eggs for breakfast. He's a phony."

Thirteen years later the traveler's train stopped again in the small New Mexico town, and he saw the same Indian sitting on the train platform. The tourist went up to him and said jovially, "How!"

The Indian answered, "Scrambled."

ᖷᓄ

Teacher: What was George Washington most famous for?
Student: His memory.
Teacher: That's an odd answer. What makes you think Washington's memory was so remarkable?
Student: Well, they sure put up a lot of monuments to it.

MENTAL PATIENTS

When a busload of people entered a large restaurant, the leader of the group approached the manager.

"Sir, I'm Mr. Phillips of the Kingsview Mental Hospital. These nice folks are mental patients in our halfway house program. They've all been cured, but they do have one small problem: They will want to pay you in bottle caps. So if you'll be so kind as to humor them in this way, I'll take care of the bill when they are through."

The manager, wanting to be a good citizen, went along and collected the bottle caps. The leader returned and with gratitude said, "Thank you so very much. I'll pay the bill now. Do you have change for a hubcap?"

MIDDLE AGE

Middle age is when you still have the old spark, but it takes more puffing.

ᖷᓄ

Maybe they call it middle age because that's where it shows first.

ᖷᓄ

Middle age is the time when your idea of getting ahead is staying even.

ᖷᓄ

Middle age is when you know all the answers and nobody asked you the questions.

∽

The hardest decision in life is when to start middle age.

∽

Middle age is when the narrow waist and the broad mind begin to change places.

MILITARY

During a practical exercise at a military police base, the instructor was giving the class instruction in unarmed self-defense. After he presented a number of different situations in which they might find themselves, he asked a student, "What steps would you take if someone were coming at you with a big, sharp knife?"
The student replied, "Big ones!"

MILK

Two local dairies engaged in an advertising war. One hired a daredevil driver to drive a car around town with a large sign reading:
THIS DAREDEVIL DRINKS OUR MILK.
The rival company came out with a larger sign reading:
YOU DON'T HAVE TO BE A DAREDEVIL TO DRINK OUR MILK.

MILKTOAST

Overpowering wife to milktoast husband: "You be quiet. When I want your opinion, I'll give it to you."

MILLION

"How many make a dozen?"
"Twelve."

"And how many make a million?"
"Very few."

MIND

"Something came into my mind just now and went away again."
"Maybe it was lonely."

⤫

"I believe I could write like Shakespeare if I had a mind to try it."
"Yes, nothing is wanting but the mind!"

MINISTER

A minister from the city was filling the pulpit in a small farm community. After his sermon he was invited over to the house of one of the members for lunch. In the course of the conversation, he mentioned with pride that his son had won first prize in the 100-yard dash.

"I know just how you must feel," declared the member understandingly. "I remember how pleased I was last year when our pig got the blue ribbon at the fair."

⤫

Little Susie, a six year old, complained, "Mother, I've got a stomachache."

"That's because your stomach is empty," the mother replied. "You would feel better if you had something in it."

That afternoon the minister called, and in conversation, remarked he had been suffering all day with a severe headache.

Susie perked up. "That's because it's empty," she said. "You'd feel better if you had something in it."

⤫

A minister named Tweedle reluctantly refused a Doctor of Divinity degree. He said that he'd rather be Tweedle dumb than Tweedle, D.D.

⤫

"How do you like the new minister?" a customer asked one of the town merchants.

"I haven't heard him preach, but I like him fine," said the merchant.

"How can you like him if you haven't heard him?"

"I know that he is good, because everyone is beginning to pay off their bills!"

∽

A minister who was very fond of pure, hot horseradish always kept a bottle of it on his dining room table. He offered some to a guest, who took a big spoonful.

When the guest finally was able to speak, he gasped, "I've heard many ministers preach hellfire, but you are the first one I've met who passed out a sample of it."

∽

An evangelist was speaking in a meeting when a heckler shouted, "Listen to him! And his father used to drive a wagon led by a donkey."

"That's right," said the evangelist, "and today my father and the wagon are gone. But I see we still have the donkey with us."

∽

A young minister, in the first days of his first parish, was obliged to call upon the widow of an eccentric man who had just died. Standing before the open casket and consoling the widow, he said, "I know this must be a very hard blow, Mrs. Vernon. But we must remember that what we see here is the husk only, the shell—the nut has gone to heaven."

∽

Visitor: How long has your minister been preaching?
Member: About thirty years.
Visitor: He ought to be through soon.

∽

A minister told his congregation that there were 739 different sins. He already has received 73 requests for the list.

∽

It was a formal banquet. The minister had just finished saying grace when a waiter spilled a bowl of steaming soup into his lap. The clergyman silently sizzled, then said in anguished tones: "Will a layman please make some appropriate remarks?"

MIRACULOUS

A traveling preacher was debating with a Texas oilman who doubted the miracle of divine chastisement. "Let me tell you of a remarkable occurrence," the preacher said. "In this morning's paper, there's an article about a politician who was struck by lightning while he was lying. Miraculous incident, wasn't it?"

"I don't know now," the Texan replied. "It would be more of a miracle if lightning struck a politician when he wasn't lying."

MISBEHAVING

Misbehaving children are youngsters whose parents embarked on the sea of matrimony without a paddle.

MISCHIEF

The chief's daughter.

MISER

"Could you tell me how you became such a rich man?"
"Turn out the lights and I will tell you the story."
"You need not tell the story. I think I already know."

MISJUDGE

A lady judge who's not married.

MISTAKE

Every married man should forget his mistakes. There is no use in two people remembering the same thing.

∽

Boss: How can one person make so many mistakes in a single day?
Employee: I get up early.

∽

A man seldom makes the same mistake twice. Generally, it's three times or more.

MONDAY

Prisoner: You mean they're going to hang me?
Guard: Yes, on Monday morning.
Prisoner: Can't you hang me on Saturday?
Guard: Why don't you want to hang on Monday?
Prisoner: Well, it seems like a terrible way to start the week.

MONEY

Things are so bad financially that one supermarket is putting in a recovery room.

∽

Doctor: Well, your examination is over and you are as sound as a dollar.
Banker: As bad as that! (And he fainted dead away!)

∽

Willard: There are thousands of ways of making money, but only one honest way.
Donald: What's that?
Willard: Ah-ha—I knew you wouldn't know!

∽

Joe: I bought this item at the fifteen-cent store.
Moe: You mean, the five-and-ten store.
Joe: Well, five and ten makes fifteen.

∽

Money doesn't go as far as it used to, but at least it goes faster.

∽

Money does make a difference. If you have two jobs and you're rich, it is called diversified interests. If you have two jobs and you're poor, you call it moonlighting.

∽

Money may talk but it seems to be very hard of hearing when you call it.

∽

The reason money is called "cold cash" is because we don't keep it long enough to get it warm.

∽

Joe: Hello, Roger, what's new?
Roger: How about that twenty dollars you owe me?
Joe: Nothing new, eh?

∽

"I want to have my face on some money."
"I would be glad if I had my hands on some."

∽

"I understand his salary goes to five figures."

"Yeah—a wife and four children."

∽

There's one advantage in being poor . . . it's very inexpensive.

∽

Most of us have two chances of becoming wealthy . . . slim and none.

∽

Hoping to develop his son's character, a father once gave his son a penny and a quarter as he was leaving for Sunday school. "Now Bill, you put whichever one you want in the offering plate," he said.

When the boy returned, his father asked which coin he had given. Bill answered, "Well, just before they sent around the plate the preacher said, 'The Lord loveth a cheerful giver,' and I knew I could give the penny a lot more cheerfully than I could give the quarter, so I gave the penny."

∽

A fellow had been standing in line to get into a movie theater. He was surprised when he reached the box office because the price for the ticket was $7.00. He pointed to a sign that said "popular prices" and said, "You call $7.00 'popular'?"

"We like it," answered the girl sweetly.

∽

Few of us can stand prosperity—another man's, I mean.

∽

I have discovered an easy way to get rich. You buy fifty female pigs and fifty male deer and put them together. Then you will have one hundred sows and bucks.

∽

Fortunate was the Wilmington lady who lost her handbag in a shopping center—an honest lad found it and returned it to her. "Funny," commented the lady, "when I misplaced the bag there was a ten dollar bill in it. Now I find ten one dollar bills."

"That's right, lady," agreed the honest lad. "The last time I found a lady's purse, she didn't have any change for a reward."

∽

Since he lost his money, half his friends don't know him anymore. And the other half? They don't know yet that he has lost it.

∽

The principal export of the United States is money.

∽

Fred: When I was twenty I made up my mind to get rich.
Carl: But you never became rich.
Fred: No. I decided it was easier to change my mind.

∽

The worst thing about history is that every time it repeats itself, the price goes up.

∽

Wife: I think you only married me because my daddy left me a lot of money.
Husband: That's not true. I didn't care who left you the money!

∽

Guru to guest: There are several meanings of life—a 50-dollar meaning, a 100-dollar meaning, and a very meaningful 500-dollar meaning.

∽

The three sons of a lawyer, a doctor, and a minister were talking about how much money their fathers made.

The lawyer's son said, "My father goes into court on a case and often comes home with as much as fifteen hundred dollars."

The doctor's son said, "My father performs an operation and earns as much as two thousand dollars for it."

The minister's son, determined not to be outdone, said, "That's nothing. My father preaches for just twenty minutes on Sunday morning, and it takes four men to carry the money."

∽

"We were so poor when I was a little boy I had to wear hand-me-down clothes!"

"So what? Everybody has to wear hand-me-downs!"

"But all I had were older sisters!"

∽

Betty: I wish I had enough money to buy an elephant.
Joe: Why do you want an elephant?
Betty: I don't. I just want the money.

∽

The man walked into the house panting and almost completely exhausted. "What happened, Honey?" inquired his wife.

"It's a great new idea I have," he gasped. "I ran all the way home behind the bus and saved fifty cents."

"That wasn't very bright," replied his wife. "Why didn't you run behind a taxi and save three dollars?"

MONKEY

"All the kids at school say I look like a monkey."

"Hush up and comb your face!"

MOONSHINE

The prosecution and defense had both presented their final arguments in a case involving a Kentucky moonshiner.

The judge turned to the jury and asked, "Before I give you your instructions, do any of you have any questions?"

"Yes, Your Honor," replied one of the jurors. "Did the defendant boil the malt one or two hours, does he cool it quickly, and at what point does he add the yeast?"

Mosquito

The mosquito has no preference,
He bites folks fat or thin.
But the welt that he raises, itches like blazes,
And that's where "the rub" comes in.

Mothers and Fathers

Mother of small boy to child psychiatrist: Well, I don't know whether or not he feels insecure, but everybody else in the neighborhood certainly does!

∽

Father: Don't you think our son gets all his brains from me?
Mother: Probably. I still have all mine.

∽

A man in a supermarket was pushing a cart which contained, among other things, a screaming baby. As the man proceeded along the aisles, he kept repeating softly, "Keep calm, George. Don't get excited, George. Don't yell, George."

A lady watched with admiration and then said, "You are certainly to be commended for your patience in trying to quiet little George."

"Lady," he declared, "I'm George!"

Mother-in-Law

Did you hear about the man who was driving down the street, when all of a sudden he came across a long line of people. They were all walking single file in the middle of the road. He drove past 100, 200, 300, until he lost count. All of them were walking single file down the yellow line in the center of the street.

Finally up ahead he saw the line slowing down to a standstill. At the head of the line he saw a hearse, and then another hearse, and then a big black limousine. The limousine had a flat tire and the driver was changing the tire. The man's curiosity was so great that he pulled his car over to the side of the road, got out, walked over to the limousine, and knocked on the window.

The window rolled down, and he saw a man in a black suit and next to him on the seat was a dog. Finally the man spoke to the fellow in the black suit. "Pardon me, sir," he said. "But I have never seen a funeral like this before. Could you tell me what is going on?"

The man in the suit replied, "Well, in the first hearse is my wife. The dog sitting next to me killed her."

"Oh, I'm terribly sorry," said the man. "But what about the second hearse?"

The man in the suit said, "In the second hearse is my mother-in-law, and the dog next to me killed her also."

"I'm so sorry," said the man. He then started to walk back to his car. About halfway there, he turned around and went back to the limousine. He said, "Excuse me, sir, but would it be possible to borrow your dog for awhile?"

(Short pause) The man in the black suit replied, "Get in line."

∽

"My mother-in-law passed away last week."
"What was the complaint?"
"There was no complaint. Everybody was satisfied."

MOTORCYCLE

Two men were traveling on a motorcycle on a windy winter day. When it became too breezy for one, he stopped and put his overcoat on backward to keep the wind from ballooning it away from him. A few miles further on, the motorcycle hit a tree, killing the driver and stunning the fellow with the reversed coat. Later, when the coroner visited the scene, he said to a rookie policeman standing nearby, "What happened?"

"Well," the officer replied, "one of them was dead when I got here, and by the time I got the head of the other one turned around, he was dead, too."

MOUNTAIN CLIMBING

Max looked up at the steep, icy mountainside. "I can't do it," he said. His companions begged him to climb the mountain with them. But he refused to move. "I'm against mountain climbing," he said.
Now they call him "Anti-climb Max."

MOUSETRAP

Young wife: Don't forget to bring home another mousetrap.
Husband: What's the matter with the one I brought yesterday?
Young wife: It's full!

MOUTH

It's better to keep your mouth shut and appear stupid than to open it and remove all doubt.

∽

To avoid trouble, breathe through your nose, and keep your mouth shut.

MOUTH FIRST

He is the only person who enters the room mouth first!

MOVIES

They show movies on the planes these days. Coming from Chicago last week, the pilot wouldn't get on. He'd already seen the picture.

∽

A mother and daughter were watching a 1930s film on TV. As it ended with the usual romantic clinch and fadeout of that era, the teenager said, "Gosh, Mom, your movies ended where ours begin."

MUGGING

Then there's the city where crime has gotten so bad that citizens figure muggings into their budgets.

MUGWUMP

One who sits on a political fence with his mug on one side and his wump on the other.

MULE

Cutting off a mule's ear won't make him a horse.

MUSTACHE

Teacher: Can any bright pupil tell me why a man's hair turns gray before his mustache?
Student: 'Cause his hair has a twenty-year head start on his mustache.

∽

Suzie: George's mustache made me laugh.
Jeanie: Yeah. It tickled me, too.

MY COUNTRY

Sometimes you wonder what kids are really learning. Yesterday a teacher pointed at the flag, turned to my six-year-old, and asked him what it was.
He answered, "It is the flag of my country."

The teacher couldn't leave well enough alone. She said, "Now tell me the name of your country."

And he said, "'Tis of Thee!"

My Wife

My wife had a terrible accident in the kitchen the other night . . . and I ate it!

〜

Joe: My wife is very touchy. The least little thing will set her off.
Moe: You're lucky. Mine is a self-starter.

〜

My wife spends a fortune on cold creams and oils—puts them all over her body. I went to grab her; she slid out of bed.

〜

My wife and I just celebrated our Tin Anniversary . . . twelve years eating out of cans.

〜

My wife will never find where I hid my extra money. I hid it in my socks that need mending!

〜

"Why are you so sad, Bill?"
"My wife said she wouldn't talk to me for thirty days."
"Why should that make you sad?"
"Today is her last day!"

〜

"My wife is always asking for money," complained a man to his friend. "Last week she wanted $200. The day before yesterday she asked me for $125. This morning she wanted $150."

"That's crazy," said the friend. "What does she do with it all?"

"I don't know," said the man, "I never give her any."

∽

My wife puts cold cream on at night, an inch thick. Then she puts those curlers in her hair, puts a fishing net over the whole thing, and says, "Kiss me."

I say, "Take me to your leader."

∽

I came home last night and there was the car in the dining room. I said to my wife, "How did you get the car in the dining room?"

She said, "It was easy. I made a left turn when I came out of the kitchen."

∽

My wife likes those little foreign cars. I bought her two . . . one for each foot.

∽

My wife changes her hair so many times she has sort of a convertible top.

∽

"I try to do everything to make my wife happy. She complained about the housework so I bought her an electric iron, an electric dishwasher, and an electric dryer. Then she complained there were so many gadgets around the house she had no room to sit down. What could I do?"

"Buy her an electric chair!"

∽

Husband: Do you think you can paint a good portrait of my wife?
Artist: My friend, I can make it so lifelike you'll jump every time you see it.

∽

She puts mud on her face before going to bed at night. I say, "Goodnight, Swamp."

∽

Bad news: Your wife has been captured by cannibals.
Worse news: They have already eaten.

∽

Keeping a secret from my wife is like trying to sneak the dawn past a rooster.

∽

My wife is just as beautiful today as when I married her twenty years ago . . . of course, it takes her longer.

∽

They say brunettes have a sweeter disposition than blondes and redheads. Don't believe it! My wife has been all three, and I couldn't see any difference.

∽

Bill: Have you heard the latest scandal?
Tom: No, my wife's out of town.

∽

Talk about an exciting weekend! Yesterday my wife and I were standing in front of a wishing well and she fell in. I didn't realize those things worked!

∽

"Was your wife outspoken?"
"Not by anyone I know of."

⌒

Did you hear about the man who asked the bellboy to carry his bag? The bellboy came over and picked up his wife.

N

Nail Polish

Q: What would you use to shine a nail?
A: Nail polish.

Nail-Biting

"I finally made my son stop biting his nails."
"How did you manage to do that?"
"I made him wear shoes."

Narrow

A narrow mind and a wide mouth usually go together.

Nasty Letter

After receiving a nasty letter, a pastor sent it back to one of his members with this note: "The enclosed letter arrived on my desk a few days ago. I am sending it to you because I think you should know that some idiot is sending out letters over your signature. Cordially . . ."

Navy

Two sailors were adrift on a raft in the ocean. They had just about given up hope of rescue. One began to pray, "O Lord, I've led a worthless life. I've been unkind to my wife and I've neglected my children, but if you'll save me, I promise . . ."
The other shouted, "Hold it. I think I see land."

A young naval student was being put through the paces by an old sea captain.

"What would you do if a sudden storm sprang up on the starboard?"

"Throw out an anchor, sir."

"What would you do if another storm sprang up aft?"

"Throw out another anchor, sir."

"And if another terrific storm sprang up forward, what would you do?"

"Throw out another anchor."

"Hold on," said the captain. "Where are you getting all those anchors from?"

"From the same place you're getting your storms, sir."

NECESSITY

Almost any luxury you see in the home of a neighbor.

NECKING

The dean of women at a large coeducational college posted an announcement that started with the sentence: "The president of the college and I have decided to stop necking on the campus."

NEIGHBOR

The Bible tells us to love our neighbors and also to love our enemies, probably because they are generally the same people.

❧

First neighbor: We are going to move. We're going to be living in a better neighborhood.

Second neighbor: So are we.

First neighbor: Oh, are you also moving?

Second neighbor: No, we're staying right here.

❧

Mrs. Brown must be offended at something. She hasn't been over for several days. Be sure to find out what it is when she does come over, and we'll try it on her again.

Neurotic

Now there's a list of the ten most neurotic people. It's called "The Best-Stressed List."

∽

My fourth husband is more neurotic than my third husband. I should have never left my third husband.

New Orleans

A number of children from the neighborhood were invited to Mrs. Johnson's for Thanksgiving dinner. She decided to do something different while serving the meal.

"Where are you originally from?" she asked one child.

"California," said the boy.

"Well then, I will give you the left wing."

She turned to another boy.

"Where are you from?"

"New York," he answered.

"You get the right wing."

She turned to the third boy. "Where are you from?"

"I'm from New Orleans and I ain't hungry."

News

Newsboy: Extra, extra! Read all about it—two men swindled.

Man: Give me one. Say, there isn't anything about two men being swindled.

Newsboy: Extra, extra! Three men swindled.

∽

Paperboy: Get your paper right here. Only fifty cents.

Out of town businessman: That's a deal. Why, back home the same paper would cost me twice as much!

Paperboy: You can pay me double if it will help you feel at home.

∽

A newsman sent a letter home from Red China. At the end he put a note: "I hope this letter reaches you. The censors are very tough." When the letter arrived, another note had been added: "There are no censors in the People's Republic of China."

NIGHT

Late-staying guest: Well, good night. I hope I have not kept you up too late.

Yawning host: Not at all. We would have been getting up soon, anyway.

NINE

Teacher: If two's company and three's a crowd, what are four and five?

Student: Nine.

NITWIT

A nitwit is a person who tells you the first half of a joke, pauses to laugh for a few minutes, and then forgets the punch line.

NO END

There are usually two sides to every argument, but no end.

NOSE

Cleopatra's nose: Had it been shorter, the whole aspect of the world would have been altered.

—*Blaise Pascal*

∽

"So you had an operation on your nose?"

"Yes, it was getting so I could hardly talk through it."

NOT HERE

Joe and Bill met on a street corner. When Joe said he sure was glad to see his friend, Bill answered, "How can you see me when I'm not even here? And I'll bet you ten dollars I can prove it!"

"You're going to bet me ten dollars you're not here? Okay, it's a bet. Go ahead and prove it."

"Am I in Chicago?"

"Nope."

"Am I in New York?"

Joe answered emphatically, "No!"

"Well, if I'm not in Chicago and I'm not in New York, that means I'm in some other place, right?"

"That's right."

"Well, if I'm in some other place, I can't be here. I'll take that ten dollars."

"How can I give you the money if you're not here?"

NOT RAISING HOGS

I Would Like to Not Raise Hogs!

(Letter sent to the Secretary of Agriculture)

Dear Mr. Secretary:

My friend Bordereaux received a $1,000 check from the government for not raising hogs and so I am going into the not-raising-hogs business.

What I want to know is, what is the best kind of land not to raise hogs on and what is the best kind of hogs not to raise? I would prefer not to raise razorbacks, but if this is not the best kind not to raise, I will just as gladly not raise Durocs or Poland Chinas.

The hardest part of this business is going to be keeping an individual record on each of the hogs I do not raise.

My friend Bordereaux has been raising hogs for more than 20 years and the most he ever made was $400 in 1918, until this year when he received $1,000 for not raising hogs. Now, if I get $1,000 for not raising 50 hogs, I assume I will get $2,000 for not raising 100 hogs, etc.

I plan to start off on a small scale, holding myself down to not raising 4,000 hogs for which I will, of course, receive $80,000.

Now these hogs I will not raise will not eat 100,000 bushels of corn. I understand you pay farmers for not raising corn. Will you pay me for not raising 100,000 bushels of corn, which I will not feed to the hogs which I am not raising?

I want to get started as soon as possible, as this looks like a good time of year for not raising hogs.

Yours very truly,
Octover Brussard

NUMBERS

If the metric system ever takes over we may have to do the following:
A miss is as good as 1.6 kilometers.
Put your best 0.3 of a meter forward.
Spare the 5.03 meters and spoil the child.
Twenty-eight grams of prevention is worth 453 grams of cure.
Give a man 2.5 centimeters and he'll take 1.6 kilometers.
Peter Piper picked 8.8 liters of pickled peppers.

Obscurity

Being the vice president of Italy.

Octopus

A cat with only eight lives left.

Offering

A minister was just about ready to go into the church for the morning service when he discovered that he could not find the offering plates. He informed the chairman of the board of deacons.

"I can't find the offering plates. I have to start the service now. See if you can find something to collect the offering in."

The chairman of the board of deacons searched for something to collect the offering in. He could not find any plates, bags, or even boxes. He thought about someone's shoes, but dismissed that as not being too dignified.

When the time came for the offering, four ushers walked down the aisle wearing broad grins and carrying shiny receptacles. The chairman had resourcefully borrowed four hubcaps from a car in the parking lot.

～

A hat was passed around a church congregation for taking up an offering for the visiting minister.

Presently it was returned to him . . . conspicuously and embarrassingly empty. Slowly and deliberately, the parson inverted the hat and shook it meaningfully. Then raising his eyes to heaven, he exclaimed fervently, "I thank thee, dear Lord, that I got my hat back from this congregation."

Oh, My Aching Back

As they left the auditorium after a two-hour lecture on nineteenth-century English poets, the wife exclaimed, "Didn't it make your mind soar?"

"Yes," her husband agreed grimly, "and my backside, too!"

Oil

Wealth that slips through your fingers.

Old

Forty is the age when a woman stops patting herself on the back and begins on the chin.

An elderly gentleman wasn't feeling well, and became irritated with his doctor because he wasn't getting better after five visits.

"Look!" said the doctor. "I'm doing all I can to help you. I can't make you younger."

"I wasn't particularly interested in getting younger," said the old man. "I just want to continue growing older."

Son: Dad, how soon will I be old enough to do as I please?
Father: I don't know. Nobody has lived that long yet.

Q: What do we call the last teeth to appear in the mouth?
A: False.

"Your age, please?" asked the census taker.

"Well," said the woman, "let me figure it out. I was 18 when I was married and my husband was 30. He is now 60, or twice as old as he was then, so I am now 36."

∽

Bill: Did you ever see a company of women silent?
Mike: Yes—when the chairman asked the oldest lady to speak first.

∽

She: Will you love me when I am old and wrinkled?
He: Yes, I do.

∽

A salesclerk asked his boss how to handle women who complained about the current prices compared to the low prices in the good old days.

"Just act surprised and tell them you didn't think that they were old enough to remember them."

∽

Patient: My right foot hurts.
Doctor: It's just old age.
Patient: But my left foot is just as old. How come it doesn't hurt?

OLD AGE

"To what do you attribute your long life?" the reporter asked the centenarian.

"I don't rightly know yet," replied the old-timer. "I'm still dickering with two breakfast food companies."

∽

The five "B's" of old age: bifocals . . . bunions . . . bridges . . . bulges . . . and baldness.

Old Days

Nothing is more responsible for the good old days than a poor memory.

Old Maid

A lady in waiting.

∽

A lady in waiting and waiting and waiting.

∽

A friend of an old maid asked her which she liked more in a man: brains, money, or appearance. The old maid responded, "Appearance—and the sooner the better."

Old-Timer

One who remembers when people who wore blue jeans worked.

∽

You're an old-timer if you remember when the only babes politicians kissed were those in their mother's arms.

∽

You are an old-timer if you remember when a babysitter was called Mother.

One Less

Husband: Well, we have a tremendous party planned for tonight. I wonder how many truly great men will be here?
Wife: There will be one less than you think.

One-Liner

A mini ha-ha.

Oops

"Thank goodness that misery is over!"
"What misery?"
"Talking with the hostess. Have you been through it yet?"
"I don't have to. I'm the host!"

∽

First man: Who is that awful-looking lady in the corner?
Second man: Why, that's my wife.
First man: Oh, I don't mean her (trying to get out of the situation), I mean the lady next to her.
Second man: That is my daughter.

Operation

Q: What is the greatest surgical operation on record?
A: Lancing Michigan.

∽

Then there is the story about the man who wanted a corn removed. The corn was painful so he went to the hospital. Since he thought the removal might be painful, he asked for an anesthetic. Once the anesthetic was applied, his heart stopped. The frantic doctors immediately operated and conducted a heart massage to revive the man.

Though the regular heartbeat was soon restored, the patient had been given such an overdose of oxygen that additional surgery was required to relieve a stomach swelling. Two operations later, the patient was being returned to the recovery room when the elevator jammed. The interns had to place him on a stretcher. During this maneuver, an intern slipped and the man crashed to the floor, breaking his arm and collarbone. The man suddenly began gasping for air. He was rushed to the operating room for his third operation of the day, a tracheotomy.

During all the confusion, the doctors forgot to remove his corn.

❧

A violinist was advised by the surgeon that he'd have to undergo an operation.

"But, doctor," intoned the patient, "I have concerts booked ahead. If you operate, can I be assured that I'll be able to play the violin in two weeks' time?"

"Undoubtedly!" assured the doctor. "The last patient on whom I performed this operation was playing a harp within twenty-four hours!"

OPINION

Writer: What do you think of my joke book? Give me your honest opinion.

Editor: It isn't worth anything.

Writer: I know, but give it to me anyway.

OPPORTUNIST

Any man who goes ahead and does what you always intended to do.

OPPOSITES

Your problem: When you take a long time to do a job, it is because you are unbearably slow and pokey.

My situation: When I take a long time, it is because I believe in quality workmanship.

❧

Your problem: When you spend your paycheck in twenty-four hours, it is because you are a spendthrift.

My situation: When I do, it is because I am generous.

❧

Your problem: When you stay in bed until 11 A.M., it is because you are a lazy, good-for-nothing.

My situation: When I stay in bed a little longer, it is because I am totally exhausted.

OPTIMIST

Q: What do they call a woman who runs the motor of her car while waiting for her husband?

A: An optimist.

∽

An optimist is someone who tells you to cheer up when things are going his way.

∽

An optimist is a fellow who grabs a fishing pole when he discovers that his basement is flooded.

∽

The optimist fell from the top story of a skyscraper. As he passed the tenth story, he was overheard muttering: "So far, so good!"

∽

A pessimist remembers the lily belongs to the onion family; an optimist that the onion belongs to the lily family.

ORATORY

The art of making deep noises from the chest that sound like important messages from the brain.

ORDER

Judge: Order in this court! I'll have order in this court!

Man: I'll have a hamburger with onions!

ORGANIZED

Don't confuse this confusion with disorganization . . . because we're not that organized yet.

OURS

Wife: And another thing I want to tell you. I've noticed every time you talk, you say my automobile, my chair, my shoes—everything's yours. You never say ours. I'm your partner. I'm your wife. It should be ours.

The husband paid no attention to his wife and just kept looking around the room for something.

Wife: What are you looking for?

Husband: Our pants.

OUTLYING

Gone to court.

OVERDRAWN

Husband: I just got a notice from the bank saying I'm overdrawn.

Wife: Try some other bank. They can't all be overdrawn.

OVERPOPULATION

Wife: This article on the overpopulation of the world says that somewhere in the world there is a woman having a baby every four seconds!

Husband: I think they ought to find that woman and stop her!

⊹ P ⊹

PAINT

Sign over bench: "Wet paint. Watch it or wear it."

PAL

Dave: I'll never forget the time we were ice skating on the lake. Suddenly the ice broke and I plunged into the water. You threw off your coat and shoes, and jumped in after me. What a pal.

Walter: What do mean, "pal"? Why wouldn't I jump in after you? You had my jacket and skates on.

PANHANDLER

A fellow walked up to a panhandler and politely remarked: "You're not too old and you're reasonably fit. Why don't you try to get a job?"

"I can't. I inherited this business from my father!"

PAPERWEIGHTS

A London street-market vendor posts this sign at his stall: "Lovely glass paperweights! The only way to keep housekeeping bills down!"

PARACHUTE JUMP

Just before a drafted farmboy made his first parachute jump, his sergeant reminded him, "Count to ten and pull the first rip cord. If it snarls, pull the second rip cord for the auxiliary chute. After you land, our truck will pick you up."

The paratrooper took a deep breath and jumped. He counted to ten, and pulled the first cord. Nothing happened. He pulled the second cord.

Again, nothing happened. As he careened crazily earthward, he said to himself, "Now I'll bet that truck won't be there either!"

PARALYZE

Two untruths.

PARKING

I solved the parking problem—I bought a parked car.

PARROT

A dignified old clergyman owned a parrot of whom he was exceedingly fond, but the bird had picked up an appalling vocabulary of cuss words from a previous owner and, after a series of embarrassing episodes, the clergyman decided he would have to kill his pet.

A lady in his parish suggested a last-ditch remedy. "I have a female parrot," she said, "who is an absolute saint. She sits quietly on her perch and says nothing but 'Let's pray.' Why don't you bring your parrot over and see if my own bird's good influence doesn't reform him."

The clergyman said it was worth a trial, and the next night he arrived with his pet tucked under his arm. The bird took one look at the lady parrot and chirped, "Hi, toots. How about a little kiss?"

"My prayers have been answered," said the lady parrot gleefully.

PARTING

Two partners had come to the parting of the ways over social and business differences.

"You stole my accounts," shouted one. "You crook."

"And you stole my wife," shouted the other. "You horse thief."

PAST TENSE

When you used to be nervous.

Pastor

The pastor of the Calvary Baptist Church in Tulsa calls this his "football theology":

Draft choice: Selection of a pew near to (or away from) air-conditioning vents.

Bench-warmer: Inactive member.

In the pocket: Where too many Christians keep their tithes.

Fumble: Lousy sermon.

Two-minute warning: Deacon in front row taking a peek at his watch in full view of the preacher.

∽

One pastor said that his church people would be the first to go up in the rapture. He gave his reason. "The Bible says, 'The dead in Christ shall rise first.'"

∽

Member: How are you feeling, pastor?

Pastor: Better.

Member: We had a committee meeting the other night and they voted to send you this get-well card. The motion passed 4 to 3!

∽

As the pastor of a local church entered the pulpit he was handed a note to be read to the congregation. The note said: "Mark Anderson having gone to sea, his wife desires the prayers of the congregation for his safety."

The pastor picked up the slip and read aloud, "Mark Anderson having just gone to see his wife, desires the prayers of the congregation for his safety."

∽

Deacon: It says here: "The wicked flee when no man pursueth."

Pastor: Yes, that is true, but they make much better time when somebody is after them.

∽

A young girl went to her pastor and confessed that she feared she had incurred the sin of vanity. "What makes you think that?" asked the minister. "Because every morning when I look into the mirror I think how beautiful I am."

"Never fear, my girl," was the reassuringly reply. "That isn't a sin, it's only a mistake."

∽

First pastor: I hear you had a revival.
Second pastor: Yes, we did.
First pastor: How many additions did you have?
Second pastor: We didn't have any additions but we had some blessed subtractions.

∽

A very foul-mouthed man met the local pastor on the street one day and said, "Now, where in hell have I seen you?" To which the pastor replied, "From where in hell do you come, Sir?"

∽

A nice but blundering old lady liked the new pastor and wanted to compliment him as she was leaving church after services. So she said to him, "I must say, Sir, that we folks didn't know what sin was until you took charge of our parish."

Pastoral Visit

A minister habitually told his congregation that if they needed a pastoral visit to drop a note in the offering plate. One evening after services he discovered a note that said: "I am one of your loneliest members and heaviest contributors. May I have a visit tomorrow evening?" It was signed by his wife.

PAUL REVERE

A Texan was trying to impress on a Bostonian the valor of the heroes of the Alamo. "I'll bet you never had anything so brave around Boston," said the Texan.

"Did you hear of Paul Revere?" asked the Bostonian.

"Paul Revere?" said the Texan. "Isn't he the guy who ran for help?"

PAY OFF

Salesman: Believe me, this sewing machine will pay for itself in no time.
Customer: Good. When it does, send it to me.

PEACEFUL COEXISTENCE

Visitors to a zoo were amazed to find a cage which was entitled "Peaceful Coexistence." It held a fox and four chickens. The zookeeper explained that it was easy to maintain the arrangement—all they had to do was to occasionally toss in a few more chickens.

PEANUT BUTTER

A bread spread.

PEARLY GATES

A minister and a congressman arrived at the pearly gates. Saint Peter greeted both of them and gave them their room assignments.

"Pastor, here are the keys to one of our nicest efficiency units. And for you, Mr. Congressman, the keys to our finest penthouse suite."

"What is the deal?" asked the minister. "This is unfair!"

"Listen," said Saint Peter, "ministers are a dime a dozen up here, but this is the first congressman we've ever seen."

PEDIATRICIAN

A man with little patients.

PEEP

He who peeps through the keyhole may lose his eye.

PENICILLIN

The best present for a man who's got everything is penicillin.

PERFECT

Preacher: Does anyone know anyone who is perfect?
A little man in the back of the church raised his hand.
Preacher: Who do you know that is perfect?
Little man: My wife's first husband.

PERFECT TIMING

Perfect timing is the ability to turn off the "hot" and "cold" shower faucets at the same time.

PERFUME

Anyone who thinks chemical warfare is something new doesn't know much about women's perfume.

PERPETUAL YOUTH

The secret of perpetual youth is to lie about your age.

Pessimist

A pessimist is always building dungeons in the air.

∽

Always borrow from a pessimist . . . he never expects it back anyhow.

∽

A pessimist is one who, when faced with two evils, chooses them both.

∽

The pessimist thinks he is taking a chance—the optimist thinks he is grasping an opportunity.

∽

A pessimist is an optimist on his way home from Las Vegas.

Pest

A person who always butts in has an infuriating complex.

Phoenicians

Sunday school teacher: What were the Phoenicians famous for?
Student: Blinds.

Phone

Teacher: If you weigh 150 pounds and you sit in the bath, what happens?
Student: The phone rings.

PHOTOGRAPH

Mary: My husband had my photograph over his heart during the war. In fact, it stopped a bullet one time and saved his life.
Jerri: I'm not surprised, dear. It would stop anything.

PHRENOLOGY

The science of picking the pocket through the scalp.

PICK

"Believe me, I pick my friends."
"Yes . . . to pieces."

PIE

Delighted by the gift she had received, the lady spoke warmly to the boy: "At church tomorrow, I'll thank your mother for this lovely pie."
"If you don't mind," the boy suggested nervously, "would you thank her for two pies?"

PIG IRON

An iron for smoothing wrinkles off pigs.

PIGEON-TOWED

There was once a beautiful fairy who yearned to be a ballet dancer. When she heard that the Royal Ballet was holding auditions in a nearby town, she harnessed one hundred white pigeons to her chariot and flew to the theater. The director took one look at her spectacular entrance and told her to go away.
"But why?" she wailed.
"Because I've got enough pigeon-towed dancers in the company already."

PIGSTY

Traveler: What does this pigsty cost?
Innkeeper: For one pig, five dollars; for two pigs, nine dollars.

PILOT

The loquacious old gentleman boarded a transport plane and started a conversation with the pilot.

"This plane takes all my courage," he said. "I was almost killed twice in an airplane."

"Once would have been enough," replied the bored pilot.

∽

"I used to be a pilot in a stable."
"That's ridiculous."
"Really, I was a pilot in a stable. I used to pilot here, pilot there . . ."

PINCH

A man and his little girl were on an overcrowded elevator. Suddenly a lady in front turned around, slapped him, and left in a huff. The little girl remarked, "I didn't like her either, Daddy. She stepped on my toe so I pinched her."

∽

As the crowded elevator descended, Mrs. Wilson became increasingly furious with her husband, who was delighted to be pressed against a gorgeous blonde.

As the elevator stopped at the main floor, the blonde suddenly whirled, slapped Mr. Wilson, and said, "That will teach you to pinch!"

Bewildered, Mr. Wilson was halfway to the parking lot with his wife when he choked, "I . . . I . . . didn't pinch that girl."

"Of course you didn't," said his wife, consolingly. "I did."

∽

"It's happened," cried the bishop in anguish as he sat playing bridge one evening with some charming people.

"What's happened?" asked the young woman next to him.

"A stroke. My left side is paralyzed."

"Are you sure?" asked the young lady.

"Yes, yes," groaned the bishop. "I've been pinching my left leg for the past few minutes and feel no sensation whatsoever."

"Relax," said the young lady. "That was my leg you were pinching."

PITCH

He who pitches too high won't get through his song.

PIZZA

Italian restaurant: "We offer you pizza and quiet."
                                        —*Bennett Cerf*

∽

Cook: Do you want me to cut this pizza into six or eight pieces?

Man: You'd better make it six. I don't think I can eat eight pieces!

PLANNING

The art of putting off until tomorrow what you have no intention of doing today.

PLEASE

Who would please all and please himself too,
Undertakes something he cannot do.

PLEASURE TRIP

First mother: I just came back from a pleasure trip.
Second mother: Where did you go?
First mother: I drove my kids to camp.

PLUM

Q: How do you tell a plum from an elephant?
A: A plum always forgets.

PNEUMONIA

What you get after you've had old monia.

POISE

The ability to be ill at ease inconspicuously.

∽

Q: What is the definition of poise?
A: The ability to keep talking while the other guy takes the check.

POLICE

John Smith happened to witness a minor holdup. In due time the police arrived, and one officer asked the witness his name.
"John Smith," said Smith.
"Cut the comedy," snapped the cop. "What's your real name?"
"All right," said Smith, "put me down as Winston Churchill."

"That's more like it," said the officer. "You can't fool me with that Smith stuff."

&

Woman: Oh, Mr. Policeman! Mr. Policeman! A man is following me and I think he is crazy!
Policeman: I agree!

&

A rookie officer was asked the following question on his examination paper: "How would you go about dispersing a crowd?"
He answered: "Take up an offering. That does it every time."

&

Joe: What kind of dog is that?
Blow: He's a police dog.
Joe: He sure doesn't look like one to me.
Blow: Of course not. He's in the secret service.

&

Q: What did the policeman say to the man with three heads?
A: Hello, hello, hello.

POLICE HELICOPTER

The whirlybird that catches the worm.

POLITICS

I like political jokes—unless they get elected.

&

"My father was a great Western politician in his day."
"Yeah? What did he run for?"
"The border."

∽

Political orator: All that I am or will be, I owe to my mother.
Heckler: Why don't you send her thirty cents and square the account?

∽

"Do you like conceited politicians as much as the other kind?"
"What other kind?"

∽

A politician is someone whose greatest asset is his liability.

∽

The deaths of politicians should always appear in the public improvement section of the newspaper.

∽

An honest politician is one who, when he is bought, will stay bought.

∽

I wish the chemists who successfully removed the lead from gasoline would try the same with our congressmen.

∽

A lobbyist browsing through an encyclopedia the other day came upon a stunning idea. In ancient Greece, in order to prevent idiot statesmen from passing stupid laws upon the people, at one point in Greek history lawmakers were asked to introduce all new laws while standing on a platform with a rope around their neck. If the law passed, the rope was removed. If it failed, the platform was removed.

∽

I stepped into the men's room once and found this sign posted over one of those hot air blowers for drying hands: "Push Button and Listen for a Short Message from the Vice President."

∾

After giving what he considered a stirring, fact-filled campaign speech, the candidate looked out at his audience and confidently asked, "Now, are there any questions?"

"Yes," came a voice from the rear. "Who else is running?"

∾

Minister: Before I vote and support you for sheriff, I'd like to know if you partake of intoxicating beverages.

Candidate for sheriff: Before I answer, tell me if this is an inquiry or an invitation.

∾

Politics is the art of looking for trouble, finding it everywhere, diagnosing it wrongly, and applying unsuitable remedies.

POLYGON

A heathen who has many wives.

POOR FAMILY

"How do you know your family was poor?"

"Every time I passed someone in town, they would say, 'There goes Joe. His poor family!'"

POP-EYED

A man sought medical aid because he had popped eyes and a ringing in the ears. A doctor looked him over and suggested removal of his tonsils. The operation resulted in no improvement, so the patient consulted another doctor who suggested removal of his teeth. The teeth were extracted but still the man's eyes popped and ringing in his ears continued.

A third doctor told him bluntly, "You've got six months to live." In that event, the doomed man decided he'd treat himself right while he could. He bought a flashy car, a chauffeur, had the best tailor in town make him 30 suits, and decided even his shirts would be made-to-order.

"Okay," said the shirtmaker, "let's get your measurements. Hmmm, 34 sleeve, 16 collar—"

"Fifteen," the man said.

"Sixteen collar," the shirtmaker repeated, measuring again.

"But I've always worn a 15 collar," said the man.

"Listen," the shirtmaker said, "I'm warning you. You keep on wearing a 15 collar and your eyes will pop and you'll have ringing in your ears."

POSITIVE

Being mistaken at the top of one's voice.

POST OFFICE

U.S. Snail

POSTDATED

A motorist driving by a Texas ranch hit and killed a calf that was crossing the road. The driver went to the owner of the calf and explained what had happened. He then asked what the animal was worth.

"Oh, about $200 today," said the rancher. "But in six years it would have been worth $900. So $900 is what I'm out."

The motorist sat down and wrote out a check and handed it to the farmer.

"Here," he said, "is the check for $900. It is postdated six years from now."

Pot Holder

A corset.

Potluck

If you believe no two women think alike, you've never been to a pot-luck dinner.

Poultry

Employee: Aren't you ashamed to give me such a poultry paycheck?
Boss: You mean paltry.
Employee: No, I mean poultry. It's chicken feed.

Power

Power will intoxicate the best hearts, as wine will the strongest heads. No man is wise enough, nor good enough, to be trusted with unlimited power.

∽

One day in the forest, three animals were discussing who among them was the most powerful.

"I am," said the hawk, "because I can fly and swoop down swiftly at my prey."

"That's nothing," said the mountain lion, "I am not only fleet, but I have powerful teeth and claws."

"I am the most powerful," said the skunk, "because with a flick of my tail, I can drive off the two of you."

Just then a huge grizzly bear lumbered out of the forest and settled the debate by eating them all . . . hawk, lion, and stinker.

Practical Jokes

A man fond of practical jokes late one night sent his friend a telegram out of a clear sky, collect, which read: I am perfectly well.

A week later the joker received a heavy parcel . . . collect . . . on which he had to pay considerable charges. On opening it, he found a big block of concrete on which was pasted this message: This is the weight your telegram lifted from my mind.

∽

Pranks for the memory.

PRAYER

The teacher handed out the test papers and told the children they could start answering the questions.

She noticed little Billy sitting with his head bowed, his hands over his face. She approached him.

"Don't you feel well?" she inquired.

"Oh, I'm fine, teacher. Maybe it's unconstitutional, but I always pray before a test!"

∽

Little William was saying his prayers one night. His mother tiptoed up and heard him say, "And please make Tommy stop throwing things at me. You may remember, I've mentioned this before. He's still doing it."

∽

A Sunday school teacher asked a little girl if she said her prayers every night.

"No, not every night," declared the child. "'Cause some nights I don't want anything!"

∽

So this big-wheel Russian is riding along when he sees a peasant kneeling in the middle of a field, praying. He stops the car, stomps over, and says:

"Aha! You waste your time like this instead of plowing and planting for the Party!"

"But, Commissar, I'm praying for the Party!"

"Praying for the Party! Huh! And years ago, you probably prayed for the Czar!"

"I did, Commissar."

"Well . . . look what happened to him!"

"Right!"

&

The pastor was invited over for dinner and asked to lead in prayer for the meal. After the brief prayer, Junior said approvingly, "You don't pray so long when you're hungry, do you?"

&

Radio prayer: Lord, comfort those who are afflicted by the radio today.

&

Mother: That's no way to say your prayers.

Daughter: But Mom, I thought that God was tired of hearing the same old stuff every night . . . so I told Him the story of the Three Bears instead.

Prayer Meeting

After attending a prayer meeting where everyone prayed very loud, a little boy remarked, "If they lived nearer to God they wouldn't have to pray so loud."

Preacher

A preacher spoke twenty minutes on Isaiah, twenty minutes on Ezekiel, twenty minutes on Jeremiah, and twenty minutes on Daniel. Then he said, "We now come to the twelve minor prophets. What place will I give Hosea?"

A man in the back of the church said, "I'm leaving. Give Hosea my place."

∽

One preacher says things are getting better because he's getting much better buttons in the collection plate.

∽

Sammy: You know what it means when a preacher steps into the pulpit, removes his watch, and places it on the pulpit?
Danny: Yeah, nothing!

∽

The new preacher, at his first service, had a pitcher of water and a glass on the pulpit. As he preached, he drank until the pitcher of water was completely gone.
After the service someone asked an old woman of the church, "How did you like the new pastor?"
"Fine," she said, "but he's the first windmill I ever saw that was run by water."

∽

Two boys were trying to outdo each other. The first said, "My uncle's a doctor. I can be sick for nothing!" The second youngster shot back, "Big deal! My uncle is a preacher. I can be good for nothing!"

∽

A parishioner had dozed off to sleep during the morning service.
"Will all who want to go to heaven stand?" the preacher asked.
All stood, except the sleeping parishioner.
After they sat down, the pastor continued: "Well, will all who want to go to the other place stand?"
Somebody suddenly dropped a songbook, and the sleeping man jumped to his feet and stood sheepishly facing the preacher. He mumbled confusedly, "Well, Preacher, I don't know what we're voting for, but it looks like you and I are the only ones for it."

Preaching

Did you hear about the minister who dreamed he was preaching a sermon and when he woke up, he was?

Prescription

Patient: You have been a great doctor. I want to leave you something in my will rather than insulting you by paying my bill.
Doctor: That's great! By the way, let me have the prescription I just gave you. I want to make a slight change in it.

ᑴᗌ

Young doctor: What is the secret of your success?
Old doctor: Always write your prescriptions illegibly and your bills very plainly.

Prince of Wales

Father: We have a new baby in our house.
Friend: I bet he reigns as king in your family now.
Father: No, Prince of Wails.

Privileged

Underprivileged: Not having remote control for your color television set.

Prodigal

A Sunday school class was being quizzed on the prodigal son. The teacher asked one youngster, "Who was sorry when the prodigal son returned home?"
The boy gave it a lot of deep thought, then said, "The fatter calf."

PROFESSION

Surgeon: I think the medical profession is the first profession mentioned in the Bible. God made Eve by carving a rib out of Adam.

Engineer: No, engineering was first. Just think of the engineering job it was to create things out of chaos.

Politician: That's nothing. Who do you think created chaos?

PROFIT

Q: What kind of money do fishermen make?
A: Net profits.

PROMISED LAND

Sunday school teacher: What do you think the "land flowing with milk and honey" will be like?
Student: Sticky!

PROMISES

First wife: Has your husband lived up to the promises he made to you before marriage?
Second wife: Just one.
First wife: Which one is that?
Second wife: He said he wasn't good enough for me.

PROPOSAL

Him: There is one word that will make me the happiest man in the world. Will you marry me?
Her: No!
Him: That's the word!

Boy: I would like to marry you.
Girl: Well, leave your name and address and if nothing better turns up, I will notify you.

❧

Daughter: Oh, Mother, please tell me if I should accept Joe's proposal.
Mother: Why don't you ask your father? He made a much smarter decision in marriage than I did.

❧

Girl one: I did not accept Jeff the first time he proposed.
Girl two: Of course not, my dear. You were not there.

PROTECTION

Son: Why is a man not allowed to have more than one wife?
Father: Because the law protects those who are incapable of protecting themselves.

PROVERB

A bright eye indicates curiosity and a black eye indicates too much curiosity.

❧

Catty remarks often have more lives than a cat.

PSYCHIATRIST

Patient: Nobody talks to me.
Psychiatrist: Next!

❧

A man went to the psychiatrist and complained about feeling inferior because of his height. The psychiatrist reminded the short fellow about the great men in history, such as Napoleon and Lautrec, who were great men in spite of their height.

The little man felt completely cured after talking to the psychiatrist and everything would have worked out fine, but as he went out of the doctor's office a cat ate him.

❦

Psychiatrist: Mr. Strange, I understand your problem is that you constantly contradict people. Right?
Patient: Wrong.
Psychiatrist: I must be mistaken then.
Patient: You are not.
Psychiatrist: Oh, I get it. You're contradicting everything I say.
Patient: That's ridiculous.
Psychiatrist: I see. Then you're perfectly sane.
Patient: Ha! I'm as crazy as a loon.
Psychiatrist: Ah, we're finally making some progress.

❦

Sign outside of psychiatrist's office: "Two Couches—No Waiting."

❦

Sign outside of psychiatrist's office: "Guaranteed Satisfaction or Your Mania Back."

❦

The patient explained to the psychiatrist that he was haunted by visions of his departed relatives.

Patient: These ghosts are perched on the tops of fence posts around my garden every night. They just sit there and watch me and watch me and watch me. What can I do?
Psychiatrist: That's easy—just sharpen the tops of the posts.

❦

Psychiatrist to patient: Did this feeling of being an insignificant person come on suddenly, or did it develop normally with marriage and parenthood?

∽

A psychiatrist is a person who beats a psychopath to your door.

∽

Patient: I'm dead.
Psychiatrist: That's impossible. You are talking to me right now.
Patient: I'm dead.
Psychiatrist: Now stand in front of that mirror and say, "Dead men don't bleed," for the next three hours.
At the end of that time the psychiatrist pricked the man's finger with a needle and it began to bleed.
Psychiatrist: There now, what does that prove?
Patient: Dead men do bleed.

∽

Patient: Doctor, I get the feeling that people don't give a hoot about anything I say.
Psychiatrist: So?

∽

Wife: You have got to help me, doctor. My husband keeps going around the house emptying ashtrays. He even does it in public places. I can't stand it!
Psychiatrist: That's not at all unusual; lots of people empty ashtrays.
Wife: Into their mouths?

∽

Psychiatrist: I have treated you for six months and now you are cured. You will no longer have delusions of grandeur and imagine that you're Napoleon.

Patient: That's wonderful. I can hardly wait to go home and tell Josephine the good news.

∽

A man went to a psychiatrist to seek some help for depression. As he entered the reception room he noticed two doors marked "Men" and "Women." He went through the door marked "Men."

He then encountered two other doors marked "Extrovert" and "Introvert." He decided that he was an introvert and opened that door. He found himself in a room with two more doors marked "Those Making $40,000 and Over" and "Those Making Less than $40,000."

He knew that he made less than $40,000, so he opened that door. He found himself outside the building.

∽

A man went to the psychiatrist because he had a fear of thunder. "Doc, I don't know what to do," said the man.

The doctor replied, "That's ridiculous. Thunder is a natural phenomenon—nothing to be afraid of. Whenever you hear thunder, do like I do: Put your head under the pillow and it will go away."

∽

The latest thing in psychiatry is group therapy. Instead of couches, they use bunk beds.

∽

His psychiatrist just told him, "You haven't got an inferiority complex. You are inferior."

∽

Psychiatrist to patient: You're quite right. A man *is* following you constantly. He's trying to collect the $200 you owe me."

∽

Psychiatrist: I'm afraid you are crazy.
Patient: Well, are you all right?
Psychiatrist: Certainly, I'm all right.
Patient: Then I'm glad I'm crazy.

∽

The psychiatrist said sternly to the patient: If you think you're walking out of here cured after only three sessions, you're crazy.

∽

I won't say he's neurotic, but last week he was watching the Army-Navy game on television and every time one of the teams went into a huddle he wondered if they were talking about him.

∽

Two psychiatrists met on the street. One smiled brightly and said, "Good morning!" The other walked on and muttered to himself, "I wonder what he meant by that!"

∽

Two eminently successful psychoanalysts occupied offices in the same building. One was forty years old, the other over seventy. They rode on the elevator together at the end of an unbearably hot, sticky day. The younger man was completely done in, and he noted with some resentment that his senior was fresh as a daisy. "I don't understand," he marveled, "how you can listen to drooling patients from morning till night on a day like this and still look so spry and unbothered when it's over."

The older analyst said simply, "Who listens?"

PSYCHOLOGIST

Dan: I'm named after my parents. My dad's name was Ferdinand and my mother's name was Liza.

Stan: What's your name, then?
Dan: Ferdiliza.

༐

"A man dropped off the eaves of this building and was killed."
"That's what he deserves for eavesdropping."

PUNISHMENT

The little young lady of the house, by way of punishment for some minor misdemeanor, was compelled to eat her dinner alone at a little table in a corner of the dining room. The rest of the family paid no attention to her presence until they heard her audibly praying over her repast with the words: "I thank thee, Lord, for preparing a table before me in the presence of mine enemies."

༐

After a family disturbance, one of the little boys closed his bedtime prayer by saying, "And please don't give my dad any more children . . . He don't know how to treat those he's got now."

༐

The prevalence of juvenile delinquency is proving that parents are not getting at the seat of the problem.

PURSE

A full purse makes the mouth run over.

⅏ Q ⅏

QUADRUPLETS

Four crying out loud.

QUAKER

A Quaker became exasperated with his cow for kicking over a pail of milk.

He warned, "Thou knowest that, because of my religion, I can't punish thee. But if thee doeth that again, I will sell thee to a Baptist preacher and he will kick thee so thee won't be able to kick it over again!"

QUESTION

He must be very ignorant for he answers every question he is asked.

⌇

He who asks a question is a fool for five minutes; he who does not ask a question remains a fool forever.

⌇

To a quick question give a slow answer.

QUESTIONS AND ANSWERS

Q: What do they call a German hippie?
A: A flowerkraut!

⌇

Q: Who invented the pendulum?
A: Pendulum Franklin.

⌇

Q: How do you keep an idiot waiting?
A: I'll tell you tomorrow.

❧

Q: Which travels faster—heat or cold?
A: Heat. . . . Because you can catch cold.

❧

Q: Where do fleas go in winter?
A: Search me.

❧

Q: What will I do if I get seasick?
A: Don't worry—you'll do it.

❧

Q: What is the best way to get to the emergency hospital?
A: Just stand out in the middle of the street.

❧

Q: How did the accident happen?
A: My wife fell asleep in the backseat.

❧

Q: How can you tell when salespeople are lying?
A: Their lips move.

❧

Q: Do you know how Yuppies wean their children?
A: They fire the maid.

❧

Q: What do sea monsters eat?
A: Fish and ships.

❧

Q: What's green, bitter, and explodes?
A: A lime bomb.

❧

Q: What is gray and stamps out jungle fires?
A: Smokey the elephant.

❧

Q: Where does a sick ship go?
A: To the doc.

❧

Q: What's black when it's clean, and white when it's dirty?
A: A blackboard.

❧

Q: What do cars do at the disco?
A: Brake dance.

❧

Q: What weighs 2,500 pounds and wears flowers in its hair?
A: A hippiepotamus.

❧

Q: What do they call a man who steals ham?
A: A hamburglar.

❧

Q: Who was Alexander Graham Bell Pulaski?
A: The first telephone Pole.

∽

Q: What's the best way to drive a baby buggy?
A: Tickle its feet.

∽

Q: What would you get if you crossed a cow with a porcupine?
A: A steak with a built-in toothpick.

∽

Q: If a rooster laid an egg on the top of a hill, which side would the egg roll down?
A: Neither side . . . a rooster can't lay eggs.

∽

Q: Why does Santa Claus have three gardens?
A: So he can ho, ho, ho.

∽

Q: What did the boy octopus say to the girl octopus?
A: I want to hold your hand hand hand hand hand hand hand hand.

∽

Q: What did one casket say to the other casket?
A: Is that you coffin?

∽

Q: On which side does a chicken have the most feathers?
A: The outside.

∽

Q: What's gray on the inside and clear on the outside?
A: An elephant in a baggie.

Q: What would you get if you crossed a flea with a rabbit?
A: A Bug's Bunny.

Q: Why do cows wear bells?
A: Because their horns don't work.

Q: What do you get when you cross a goat and an owl?
A: A hootenanny.

Q: What do fish sing to each other?
A: Salmon-chanted Evening.

Q: Where did the whale go when it was almost bankrupt?
A: He went to see the loan shark.

Q: Where did Noah keep the bees?
A: In the arkives.

Q: What do you get if you cross a hyena with aman-eating tiger?
A: I don't know, but if it laughs you'd better join in.

Q: Why do welders work such long hours?
A: Because they find their work so riveting.

∽

Q: What is very quiet and explodes?
A: A mime bomb.

∽

Q: What do you call a man who can't stop buying carpets?
A: A rug addict.

∽

Q: How would you send a message to a shark?
A: Drop it a line.

∽

Q: What did they call the canary that flew into the pastry dish?
A: Tweetie Pie.

∽

Q: Who are all the fish of the sea afraid of?
A: Jack the Kipper.

∽

Q: What's the largest thing ever made of grapes?
A: The Grape Wall of China.

∽

Q: How does a monster count to fourteen?
A: On his fingers.

∽

Q: Which famous comedian sacked Rome?
A: Attila the Fun.

QUININE

A valuable medicine that comes from barking trees.

QUOTABLE QUOTES

If a politician tries to buy votes with private money, he is a dirty crook; but if he tries to buy them with the people's own money, he's a great liberal.

∽

Many a child who watches television for hours will go down in history, not to mention arithmetic, English, and geography.

∽

People seldom think alike until it comes to buying wedding presents.

∽

A halo has only to fall eleven inches to become a noose.

∽

A man's horse sense deserts him when he is feeling his oats.

∽

Confucius say, ostrich who keep head in sand too long during hot part of day gets burned in end.

∽

He charged nothing for his preaching, and it was worth every penny of it.

∽

What this country needs is a good five-cent nickel.

∽

I do most of my work sitting down; that is where I shine.

∽

Running into debt doesn't bother me; it's running into my creditors that's upsetting.

∽

Many of our ambitions are nipped in the budget.

❧ R ❧

RACEHORSE

A racehorse can take several thousand people for a ride at the same time.

RAGMAN

Wife: There's an old-clothes man at the door.
Husband: Tell him I've got all the clothes I need.

RAIN CHECKS

A visitor to a drought-stricken area was engaged in conversation at the local store about the "no-rain" situation.

"You think the drought is bad here," the merchant observed, "but down south o'here a-ways, they haven't had any for so long that the Baptists are sprinkling, the Methodists are using a damp cloth, and the Presbyterians are issuing rain checks!"

RAISE

Employee: Sir, my wife . . . er . . . told me I must ask for an increase.
Employer: Well, I'll ask my wife if I can give you one.

☙

Employee (shaking a little): Could I have a raise?
Manager: You can't come in here like this and ask for a raise. You have only been with the company two weeks. You have to work yourself up first.
Employee: But I did . . . look . . . I'm trembling all over!

☙

"I am planning a salary increase for you, young man."
"When does it become effective?"
"Just as soon as you do!"

RAMPAGE

The page in the encyclopedia about male sheep.

RANSOM

Kidnapper: Lady, we are going to hold you until your husband ransoms you.

Woman: Oh, dear. I wish now that I had treated William a little better.

RATTAN

What a rat gets while vacationing in Florida.

RAZOR

Jim: I got one of those new razors that has twin blades.
Tom: How do you like it?
Jim: Shaves good. But now instead of getting nicks, I get ditto marks.

READING

Librarian: Please be quiet. The people next to you can't read.
Boy: What a shame! I've been reading since I was six.

REAL PANE

A preacher was called upon to substitute for the regular minister, who had failed to reach the church because he was delayed in a snowstorm. The speaker began by explaining the meaning of a substitute. "If you break a window," he said, "and then place a piece of cardboard there, that is a substitute."

After the sermon, a woman who had listened intently shook hands with him, and wishing to compliment him, said, "You were no substitute. You were a real pane!"

REALTORS

Realtors . . . you have lots to be thankful for.

RECEPTION COMMITTEE

About three weeks before an annual club dinner, a member received a letter from the club president, asking him to serve on the reception committee and be there at seven o'clock sharp. A scarlet ribbon marked RECEPTION COMMITTEE was enclosed. He hadn't meant to go. The dinners were usually a bore. But since he had been asked to be on the committee, he decided to go.

By the time he arrived, almost all eight hundred members of the club were there, each wearing a scarlet ribbon marked RECEPTION COMMITTEE.

RECKLESS DRIVER

One who is seldom wreckless for long.

RECOVERY

On August 7, 1990, the old gentleman suffered a stroke, but with the loving care of his family and his kind and efficient nurse, he never fully recovered.

REDEMPTION

A man wanted to arrange for the disposal of a $5,000 bond, so he called his bank.

"Sir," said the clerk, "is the bond for redemption or conversion?"

After a long pause the man said, "Well, am I talking to the First National Bank or the First Baptist Church?"

REDUCE

The only sure way to reduce is to set the bathroom scale in front of the refrigerator.

REFERENCE

Letter of reference: This employee has worked for me for one week and I am satisfied.

REGRET

Husband: If a man steals anything, he will live to regret it.

Wife: You used to steal kisses from me before we were married.

Husband: Well . . .

RELATIVES

One of the great mysteries of life is how that idiot who married your daughter can be the father of the smartest grandchildren in the world.

RELAX

The time to relax is when you don't have time for it.

RELIGIOUS FREEDOM

To some people religious freedom means the choice of churches that they may stay away from.

REMEMBER

A worker was called on the carpet by his supervisor for talking back to his foreman. "Is it true that you called him a liar?"

"Yes, I did."

"Did you call him stupid?"

"Yes."

"And did you call him an opinionated, bullheaded egomaniac?"

"No, but would you write that down so I can remember it?"

∽

An elephant never forgets, but what has he got to remember?

RENT

Bill: How much are they asking for your apartment rent now?

Bob: About twice a day.

REPENTANCE

Most people repent their sins by thanking God they ain't so wicked as their neighbors.

—Josh Billings

∽

It is much easier to repent of sins that we have committed than to repent of those that we intend to commit.

—Josh Billings

REPORT CARD

Son: Here's my report card, Dad, along with one of your old ones I found in the attic.

Father: Well, Son, you're right. This old report card of mine you found isn't any better than yours. I guess the only fair thing to do is give you what my father gave me.

∽

A father was examining his son's report card. "One thing is definitely in your favor," he announced. "With this report card, you couldn't possibly be cheating."

REPOSE

Whilst Adam slept, Eve from his side arose:
Strange his first sleep should be his last repose.

RESEMBLANCE

"Who is that homely boy who just walked into the room?"
"Why, that's my brother!"
"Oh, you must excuse me. I really hadn't noticed the resemblance."

RESORT

Place where people go for change and the landlord gets the rest.

REST

"My uncle was finally put to rest last week."
"I didn't know that he had passed away."
"He didn't, but my aunt did."

RESTITUTION

A home for chronically exhausted people.

RETORT

"Why darling, I was just wondering why you weren't invited to the party the Smiths had last week!"

"Isn't that a coincidence. I was just wondering why you were!"

∽

"The president has personally asked me to help beautify the United States on a special project."

"Really? And which country have you decided to move to?"

∽

Actor: As a matter of fact, I have received letters from ladies in almost every place in which I have appeared.

Rival: Landladies, I presume.

RETURN TO SENDER

A bookseller had a statement for a book curtly returned to him with this note written across it:

"Dear Sir: I never ordered this beastly book. If I did, you didn't send it. If you sent it, I never got it. If I got it, I paid for it. If I didn't, I won't!"

REVENGE

Did you hear about the man who burned the farmer's sugarcane field because he wanted sweet revenge?

∽

The twelve-year-old boy stood patiently beside the clock counter while the druggist waited on all of the adult customers. Finally he got around to the youngster, who made his purchase and hurried out to the curb, where his father was impatiently waiting in his car.

"What took you so long in there, son?" he asked.

"The man waited on everybody in the store before me," the boy replied. "But I got even."

"How?"

"I wound all the alarm clocks while I was waiting," the youngster explained happily. "It's going to be a mighty noisy place at eight o'clock."

REVERSE REASON

She married him because he was such a "dominating man"; she divorced him because he was such a "dominating male."

He married her because she was so "fragile and petite"; he divorced her because she was so "weak and helpless."

She married him because "he knows how to provide a good living"; she divorced him because "all he thinks about is business." He married her because "she reminds him of his mother"; he divorced her because "she's getting more like her mother every day."

She married him because he was "happy and romantic"; she divorced him because he was "shiftless and fun-loving."

He married her because she was "steady and sensible"; he divorced her because she was "boring and dull."

She married him because he was "the life of the party"; she divorced him because "he never wants to come home from a party."

RICE

A product associated with the worst mistake of some men's lives.

RICH MAN

One who isn't afraid to ask the clerk to show him something cheaper.

RIDICULE

Ridicule is the first and last argument of fools.

RIGHT

Boss: What do you mean by arguing with that customer? Don't you know our rule? The customer is always right.

Employee: I know it. But he insisted that he was wrong.

RIGHTS

A man is endowed with certain inalienable rights, all of which he must fight for.

RIP VAN WINKLE

A modern-day Rip Van Winkle slept for twenty years. Upon awaking he immediately called his broker.

"What's the stock market done the past twenty years?" he inquired.

With the aid of a computer, his broker soon was able to report that his one hundred shares of AT&T were now worth $9.5 million, his one hundred shares of General Motors worth $7.9 million, and his oil holdings had increased to $19 million.

"Great!" Rip exclaimed, "I'm rich!"

At which point the telephone operator interrupted and said, "Your three minutes are up, sir. Would you please deposit a million dollars?"

ROBBED

The teller had just been robbed for the third time by the same man, and the police officer was asking if he had noticed anything specific about the criminal.

"Yes," said the teller, "he seems to be better dressed each time."

ROCK FESTIVAL

I went to a rock festival last summer and it was fascinating. There were four hundred girls, five hundred boys and fifty uncommitted.

ROME

Teacher: When was Rome built?
Student: It was built during the night.
Teacher: The night? Where did you ever get such an idea?
Student: Well, everyone knows that Rome wasn't built in a day.

ROOKIE

First rookie: I feel like punching that sarge in the nose again!
Second rookie: What do you mean, *again?*
First rookie: Well, I felt like it yesterday, too.

ROOT BEER

Did you hear about the fellow who spilled some root beer on the stove?
Now he has foam on the range.

ROSE

Carl: What's that you have in your buttonhole?
Earl: Why, that's a chrysanthemum.
Carl: It looks like a rose to me.
Earl: Nope, you're wrong. It's a chrysanthemum.
Carl: Spell it.
Earl: K-r-i-s . . . by golly, that is a rose.

ROUND

Ruth: Where did Walter go?
Julie: He's 'round in front.
Ruth: I know what he looks like, I just wanted to know where he went.

RUBBER TREES

Stretch plants.

RULE

First husband: Do you agree with the prediction that women will be
ruling the world in the year 2000?
Second husband: Yes, they will still be at it.

RUMOR

What dainty morsels rumors are. They are eaten with great relish!

∽

A flying rumor never has any trouble in making a landing.

RUSH HOUR

When the traffic stands still.

RUSSIANS

I hear they're putting up a $20,000,000 hotel right in the heart of Moscow. Gonna call it the "Comrade Hilton."

∽

Russian economist: I went over to the United States to study the death of capitalism.
Russian leader: What are your conclusions?
Russian economist: What a wonderful way to die.

∽

No wonder the Russians are getting so confident. If they've been watching television, they might figure every American has either tired blood, indigestion, or nagging headaches.

✢ S ✢

SALESMAN

Shoe salesman who had dragged out half his stock to a woman customer: Mind if I rest a few minutes, lady? Your feet are killing me.

∾

"This house," said the real estate salesman, "has both its good points and its bad points. To show you I'm honest, I'm going to tell you about both. The disadvantages are that there is a chemical plant one block south and a slaughterhouse a block north."

"What are the advantages?" inquired the prospective buyer.

"The advantage is that you can always tell which way the wind is blowing."

∾

Sales clerk: Those eggs just came from the country.
Shopper: What country?

∾

A man walked into a men's clothing store and told the manager he wanted a job as a salesman.

"Sorry, we don't need any salesmen," the manager told him.

"But you've just got to hire me," the man said. "I'm the world's greatest salesman!"

The sales manager again refused, but the man hung on and was so convincing that finally the manager said, "Okay, I'll tell you what I'll do. See that suit over there hanging on the back wall? After you've dusted it off, you'll see that it has padded shoulders, pointed lapels, and a belt in the back. It's sort of a blue-orange-green-purple plaid. I don't even remember how I got stuck with it. Now, I'm going to lunch and I'm going to leave you in charge. If you can sell that suit before I get back, you're hired."

About an hour later the manager returned to find the store in a mess. The rugs were ripped, a showcase was turned over, and merchandise was all over the floor, but the suit was gone.

"Well, I see you've sold the suit."

"Yes, Sir."

"It looks like you had a little trouble with the customer, though."

"No, Sir. Not a bit of trouble with the customer—but oh, that seeing-eye dog."

SAWMILL

Ken: I slept like a log.

Melba: Yes, I heard the sawmill.

SCHOOL DAYS

Teacher: If your mother gave you a large apple and a small one, and told you to divide them with your brother, which would you give him?

Johnnie: Do you mean my little brother or my big brother?

ᴄᴏ

The teacher told my mother I was a flathead. She was so thrilled that she went all around the neighborhood and bragged about my being so levelheaded.

ᴄᴏ

Father: I see you got a D for conduct but an A for courtesy. How is that possible?

Son: Whenever I kick someone I apologize.

ᴄᴏ

Student: I've just had a brilliant idea.

Teacher: It's probably beginner's luck.

ᴄᴏ

As a special treat, a teacher took her class to visit the museum of natural history. The children returned home excitedly, and on rushing into his house one of the little boys greeted his mother exuberantly. "What do you think we did today, Mother? The teacher took us to a dead circus."

༄

Student: I don't think I deserve a zero on this test!
Teacher: Neither do I, but it's the lowest mark I can give you.

༄

Teacher: If you cut an apple into four pieces it is called quarters. And if you slice it into eight pieces it is called eighths. What is it called when you slice it into eight thousand parts?
Student: Applesauce.

༄

Teacher: What is an emperor?
Scholar: I don't know.
Teacher: An emperor is a ruler.
Scholar: Oh, sure; I used to carry an emperor to school with me.

༄

Teacher: Billy, what did you do when Ed called you a liar?
Billy: I remembered what you told me: "A soft answer turns away anger."
Teacher: Very good, Billy. What answer did you give him?
Billy: I answered him with a soft tomato.

༄

Teacher: What is the axis of the earth?
Student: The axis of the earth is an imaginary line which passes from one pole to the other, and on which the earth revolves.
Teacher: Very good. Now, could you hang clothes on that line?
Student: Yes, Sir.

༄

Teacher: Indeed, and what sort of clothes?
Student: Imaginary clothes, Sir.

∾

Teacher: How much is six and four?
Student: That's about eleven, ain't it?
Teacher: Six and four are ten.
Student: Six and four couldn't be ten, because five and five are ten.

∾

A school boy took home a library book whose cover read *How to Hug,* only to discover that it was Volume VII of an encyclopedia!

∾

Girl: Too bad you flunked the test. How far were you from the right answer?
Boy: Two seats!

∾

Father: Why are you always at the bottom of your class?
Dennis: It doesn't make any difference. They teach the same thing at both ends.

∾

Teacher: I hope I didn't see you looking at someone else's paper, Billy.
Billy: I hope so, too, Teacher.

∾

Here's my report card . . . and I'm tired of watching TV anyway.

∾

Teacher: How fast does light travel?
Student: I'm not sure, but I do know it always gets here too early in the morning.

∾

Teacher: Name the four seasons.
Student: Pepper, salt, vinegar, and mustard.

❧

Teacher: Johnny, if your father earned one hundred dollars a week and gave your mother half, what would she have?
Johnny: Heart failure.

SCOTCHMAN

Clerk: Sir, there's a Scotchman at the counter who wants to buy ten cents worth of poison to commit suicide. Is there something I can do to save him?
Store owner: Tell him it will cost twenty cents.

❧

McTavish: A fellow walked up to me today and asked for a nickel for a cup of coffee. I gave it to him and then followed him clear across town to the restaurant.

❧

A Scotsman and an Englishman were leaning against the counter in a store when a bandit walked in and brandished his gun.
The Scot, a quick thinker, hauled out his money and handed it to his English friend.
He said, "Here's the ten dollars you lent me."

❧

There was once a Scotchman who had played golf with the same ball for thirty years. One day he lost it and was forced to buy another. He walked into the local sports shop and said, "Well, here I am again."

Sermon

Pastor: Isn't this a beautiful church? Here is a plaque for the men who died in the service.
Man: which one—morning or evening?

☙

A minister preached a very short sermon. He explained, "My dog got into my office and chewed up some of my notes."
At the close of the service a visitor asked, "If your dog ever has pups, please let my pastor have one of them."

☙

First member: I thought the sermon was divine. It reminded me of the peace of God. It passed all understanding.
Second member: It reminded me of the mercies of God. I thought it would endure forever.

Ship

Q: What is the difference between valor and discretion?
A: To travel on an ocean liner without tipping would be valor. To come back on a different ocean liner would be discretion.

☙

Willy: That boat did twenty-five miles per hour.
Billy: Twenty-five miles? You mean knots.
Willy: Well, miles to me, knots to you.

Signs of the Times

Sign on garbage truck:
SATISFACTION GUARANTEED, OR DOUBLE YOUR GARBAGE BACK.

☙

Sign on wishing well:
WISH CAREFULLY. NO REFUNDS.

∽

Sign outside house in the city:
TRESPASSERS WILL BE PROSECUTED TO THE FULL
EXTENT OF ONE GERMAN SHEPHERD.

∽

Sign on bankrupt store:
OPENED BY MISTAKE.

∽

Sign in a reducing-salon window:
WE CAN TAKE YOUR BREADTH AWAY.

∽

Misprint on sign at drugstore:
YOU CAN BE SURE OF HAVING YOUR PRESCRIPTIONS
FILLED WITH SCARE AND KILL.

∽

Sign in laundry window:
WE DO NOT TEAR YOUR LAUNDRY WITH MACHIN-
ERY, WE DO IT BY HAND.

∽

Sign in restaurant:
IF YOU ARE OVER 80 AND ACCOMPANIED BY YOUR
PARENTS, WE WILL CASH YOUR CHECK.

∽

Sign on the Los Angeles boundary line:
YOU HAVE JUST LEFT THE CITY OF LOS ANGELES.
RESUME NATURAL BREATHING.

∽

A sign on a dryer in a coin laundry reads:
THIS DRYER IS WORTHLESS.
A sign on the next dryer reads:
THIS DRYER IS NEXT TO WORTHLESS.

SHORTENING

Larry: You told me if I rubbed grease on my chest I'd grow tall like you, but it didn't work.
Harry: What did you use?
Larry: Crisco.
Harry: Stupid; that's shortening.

SIDE

Sir, my concern is not whether God is on our side; my great concern is to be on God's side, for God is always right.

SINGING

The choir had come out of rehearsal.
"Am I to assume that you do a lot of singing at home?" Bill Garrison asked a fellow choir member, Roy Greene.
"Yes, I sing a lot. I use my voice just to kill time," said Roy.
Bill nodded, "You certainly have a fine weapon."

∽

Fan: You certainly sang "Lilacs in the Rain" beautifully. You sang the words so well I could smell the lilacs.

Singer: The words? What about my singing?
Fan: I could smell that, too.

∽

Wife: Did you notice how the opera singer's voice filled the hall?
Husband: Yes. I also noticed that a lot of people left to make room
for it.

∽

Mark: How about a song?
Ryan: Who, me?
Mark: Yeah.
Ryan: Not me. I only do my singing in the shower.
Mark: Don't sing very often, do you?

SLAPPED

The story is told of a young Czechoslovakian man, a Russian officer,
a little old lady, and an attractive young woman riding on a train.

Shortly after the train entered a dark tunnel, the passengers heard a
kiss, then a loud slap.

The young woman thought: "Isn't that odd the Russian tried to kiss
the old lady and not me?"

The old lady thought: "That is a good girl with fine morals."

The Russian officer thought: "That Czech is a smart fellow; he steals
a kiss and I get slapped."

The Czech thought: "Perfect. I kiss the back of my hand, clout a
Russian officer, and get away with it."

SMILE

To make a smile come, so they say,
brings 15 muscles into play.
But if you want a frown to thrive
you have to use some 65.

SMOGARIA

Q: What's the difference between a Smogarian grandmother and an elephant?
A: About seven pounds.

☙

Dope ring? . . . that's twelve Smogarians sitting in a circle.

☙

Q: Why don't Smogarians kill flies?
A: It's their national bird.

☙

"Did you hear about the Smogarian orchestra that stopped in the middle of a performance to clean the saliva out of their instruments?"
"What's wrong with that?"
"This was a string orchestra."

☙

Q: What is gross stupidity?
A: One hundred, forty-five Smogarians.

☙

Q: What does it say on the bottom of Coke bottles in Smogaria?
A: Open the other end.

☙

Q: How much does a Smogarian pay for a haircut?
A: Four dollars—a dollar for each side.

☙

Q: How do you make a Smogarian shish kebab?
A: Shoot an arrow into a garbage can.

∽

Q: Why do Smogarians have scratched faces on Monday morning?
A: Because they eat with knives and forks over the weekend.

∽

Q: What do they call a group of Smogarian paratroopers?
A: Air pollution.

∽

Q: How did the employer of a large company know that he had hired a Smogarian secretary?
A: There was white-out all over the computer screen.

∽

Q: Why did the Smogarian big-game hunter give up hunting for elephants?
A: He got tired carrying around the decoys.

∽

Q: What happened to the Smogarian when he learned that he had been promoted from second grade to third grade?
A: He was so excited that he cut himself while shaving.

∽

Q: What do you call a Smogarian who practices birth control?
A: A humanitarian.

∽

Q: What do you call an attractive woman in Smogaria?
A: A tourist.

∽

Q: Why were the Smogarians so excited when a new bridge was built across one of their widest rivers?
A: Because they could swim across the river in the shade.

$\backsim$

Q: Why do Smogarians drink less Kool-Aid than other folks?
A: Because they have such a hard time getting two quarts of water into those little envelopes.

$\backsim$

Did you hear about the Smogarian who thought that radioactivity was an exercise program on the radio?

$\backsim$

Did you hear about the two Smogarians who were building a house? One of them kept throwing away half of the nails.
"What's the matter?" said the other Smogarian.
"About half of these nails have the head on the wrong end."
"You fool," said the other Smogarian. "Those are for the other side of the house."

$\backsim$

Did you hear about the two Smogarians who committed a bank robbery? As they sped down the road one of the Smogarians said, "Look behind us and see if the cops are following us."
"How will I know?" said the other Smogarian.
"They will have their flashing red lights on."
"Do you see any of the police following us?"
"Yes...No...Yes...No...Yes...No...Yes...No...Yes..."

$\backsim$

Teacher: What shape is the earth?
Smogarian: I dunno.
Teacher: Well, what kind of earring does your girlfriend wear?

Smogarian: Square ones.
Teacher: No, I mean the ones she wears on Sunday.
Smogarian: Round.
Teacher: Then, what shape is the earth?
Smogarian: Square on weekdays and round on Sundays.

∽

Did you hear about the two Smogarians who were hunting in the woods? Before long, they realized that they were lost and could not get back to civilization.

"Don't worry," one of them said. "When you're lost in the woods, all you have to do is fire three shots in the air."

They did so and waited. An hour later they did it again, and still no one came. Finally they tried a third time.

"This had better work," the other Smogarian said. "These are our last arrows."

∽

Q: How do Smogarian fishermen count the daily catch of fish?
A: One fish . . . two fish . . . another fish . . . another fish . . . another fish . . .

∽

Q: What do you call a Smogarian with half a brain?
A: Gifted.

∽

Q: What is the smallest building in Smogaria?
A: The Hall of Fame.

∽

Q: Why are Smogarian mothers so strong?
A: It comes from raising dumbbells.

∽

Q: What do you have when you extend the first finger of your right hand?

A: A Smogarian handkerchief.

SMOKING

Jay: Does the Bible say that if you smoke you can't get to heaven?
Bufe: No, but the more you smoke the quicker you'll get there.

∽

Smoking a cigarette won't send you to hell. It just makes you smell like you've been there.

∽

There is a new cigarette with earplugs in every pack. It's for people who don't want to hear why they should quit smoking.

∽

"Will my smoking this cigar bother you?"
"Not if my getting sick won't bother you!"

SOAP

First lady: Just look at this. I have managed to entirely furnish one of the rooms in our house by collecting soap coupons.
Second lady: Aren't you going to furnish the other six rooms?
First lady: I can't. They're full of soap.

SPANKING

Stern punishment.

∽

Father: Now, remember, I'm spanking you because I love you.
Son: I sure wish I was big enough to return your love.

Speaker

I have been told that the mind cannot absorb any more than the seat can endure.

His ideas are sound—all sound.

He was such a bad speaker the audience hissed the ushers.

I have the microphone and there is the loud speaker!

And now I'm going to say something in the public interest . . . Good-night.

I spoke to a group of hippies and they're a tough audience. They don't laugh or applaud . . . they're too busy scratching!

Sign on speaker's table: "If you don't strike oil in twenty minutes, stop boring."

Every time I stand up to speak my mind sits down!

That was the sort of speech that gives failure a bad name.

☙

In biblical days, it was considered a miracle when a donkey spoke. Listening to him you can't help but realize how times haven't changed.

☙

After a dinner program like this, a speaker is like parsley—not really needed.

☙

Chancey Depew once played a trick on Mark Twain on an occasion when they were both to speak at a banquet. Twain spoke first for some twenty minutes and was received with great enthusiasm. When Depew's turn came immediately afterward, he said, "Mr. Toastmaster, Ladies and Gentlemen, before this dinner, Mark Twain and I made an agreement to trade speeches. He has just delivered mine and I'm grateful for the reception you have accorded it. I regret that I have lost his speech and cannot remember a thing he had to say."

He sat down with much applause.

☙

Two speakers were on the same program. One of them did an outstanding job of delivery. The other speaker was boring. The boring speaker was overheard saying, "Poor Dr. Wilson, he's having it pretty rough. He spoke before I did and he didn't go over at all. In fact, the crowd didn't like him—they booed and hissed the poor fellow right off the stage. He was so bad that right in the middle of my speech, they started booing him again!"

☙

"Thank you for the privilege of speaking to you in this magnificent auditorium. You know the meaning of the word 'auditorium,' don't you? It is derived from two Latin words . . . audio, to hear, and taurus, the bull."

☙

After a great host of boring speakers had spoken, the last speaker rose to the platform clutching a bulky prepared speech. The guests could hardly conceal their restlessness. However, he made many friends when he said, "Friends, it's so late I've decided to just mail each of you a copy of this speech." Then he bowed and sat down.

After the dinner is over,
After the waiters have gone,
After the coffee and mint-drops,
After the very last song;
Then come the speeches and laughter,
And we settle ourselves for a Coke,
In the hope that one of the speakers
Will tell us a really good joke.

A distinguished man was invited to a banquet to speak. When he arrived he was placed at the head table. Next to him was an empty chair. The speaker placed his hat on the chair.

A little later, a rather large lady came to the table, pulled out the chair and sat on the speaker's hat. It was crushed as flat as a pancake.

The speaker turned to the woman and said, "Madam, I could have told you that my hat would not fit before you tried it on."

"He made an unusually good after-dinner speech."
"What did he say?"
"He said, 'Waiter, give me the check.'"

He gave a tremendous speech. Everyone was moved . . . toward the exit.

Speaker: Yes, my audiences are glued to their seats when I speak.
Bored listener: What a quaint way of keeping them there.

∽

Delivering a speech at a banquet on the night of his arrival in a large city, a visiting minister told several anecdotes he expected to repeat at meetings the next day. Because he wanted to use the jokes again, he requested the reporters to omit them from any accounts they might turn in to their newspapers. A cub reporter, in commenting on the speech, ended his piece with the following: "The minister told a number of stories that cannot be published."

∽

A chauffeur-driven Cadillac pulled up in front of our auditorium . . . stopped with a jerk . . . and out came our speaker of the evening.

∽

"He's such a great speaker. I'd rather hear him speak than eat."
"Me, too. I sat at the head table with him. I've heard him eat."

∽

I would like to present the funniest, most talented, most outstanding speaker and the fellow who wrote this introduction for me . . .

SPECTACLES

Wife: What about spectacles?
Husband: Spectacles are glasses that people look through.
Wife: If you looked through a window would you call it a spectacle?
Husband: It depends on what you saw.

SPEECH

A wise man once said that the best way to save face is to keep the bottom part of it closed.

∽

Upon entering a room in a hotel, a woman recognized a well-known government official pacing up and down and asked what he was doing there. "I am going to deliver a speech," he said.

"Do you usually get very nervous before addressing a large audience?"

"Nervous?" he replied. "No, I never get nervous."

"In that case," demanded the lady, "what are you doing in the ladies' room?"

∽

World's Best After-Dinner Speech: "Waiter, give me both checks."

SPEECH LESSONS

In order to become a good speaker, you must go to diction school. They teach you how to speak clearly. To do this, they fill your mouth with marbles and you're supposed to talk clearly right through the marbles. Now every day you lose one marble. When you've lost all your marbles . . .

∽

"You heard my speech, Professor. Do you think it would improve my delivery if I followed the example of Demosthenes and practiced my diction and elocution with pebbles and marbles in my mouth?"

"I would recommend quick-dry cement."

SPELLING

Joe: Why did you fire your secretary?

Moe: She couldn't spell. She kept asking me how to spell every other word as she was taking dictation.

Joe: I suppose you couldn't stand the interruptions.

Moe: It wasn't that. I just didn't have time to look up all those words.

∽

Employer: How's your spelling? Let me hear you spell Mississippi.

Secretary: The river or the state?

∽

First boy: I couldn't learn to spell.
Second boy: Why not?
First boy: My teacher always changed the words.

SPINSTER

A woman who is unhappily unmarried.

∽

First spinster: Why did you sell your double bed and buy twin beds?
Second spinster: Because every night I look under the bed to see if a man is there. With two beds, my chances are doubled.

SPLINTERS

Chet: How did you get your hand full of splinters?
Jack: I was out hunting and caught a timber wolf barehanded.

SPORTING

"I hear your husband is a linguist."
"Yes. He speaks three languages . . . golf, football, and baseball."

∽

"If you're such a good fortune-teller, you should be able to tell me the score of tonight's hockey game before it starts!"
"Before the game starts, the score will be nothing to nothing!"

∽

Bob: The national sport in Spain is bullfighting and in England it's cricket.
Ray: I'd rather play in England.
Bob: Why do you say that?
Ray: It's easier to fight crickets.

∽

There was a hitchhiker walking down the road. A young man passed by in a sports car and asked, "Do you want to drag?"

So the hitchhiker started running and the young man speeded up to sixty miles an hour, looked back and saw the hitchhiker. The driver speeded up to 100 m.p.h. and the hitchhiker was still running behind him. Then the driver speeded up to 120 m.p.h. and the hitchhiker disappeared from sight.

The driver decided to turn back and find the hitchhiker to see what happened. There was the hitchhiker lying exhausted in a ditch.

"What happened?" asked the driver.

"You'd blow out a tennis shoe, too, if you were going 120 m.p.h.," said the hitchhiker.

∽

The trouble with being a good sport is that you have to lose to prove it.

∽

"Did you hear about the cross-eyed discus thrower?"
"No, did he set lots of records?"
"No, but he sure kept the crowd alert!"

∽

A coach was being congratulated on having a lifetime contract. "I guess it's all right," he said. "But I remember another guy with a lifetime contract. Had a bad year, and the president called him in, pronounced him dead, and fired him."

∽

I used to box. My best punch was a rabbit punch, but they would never let me fight rabbits.

∽

Q: What did the man say when he lost the fencing match?
A: Foiled again.

∽

Boxing coach: You did a terrible job out there. If I were as big as you, I would be heavyweight champion of the world.

Boxer: Why don't you become the lightweight champion?

∽

"The reason I climb mountains is because they are there!"

"That's the reason everybody else goes around them!"

∽

Those who exercise regularly, die healthier.

∽

Lady at the store: I am a physical education teacher and I would like to buy a pair of shorts to wear around my gymnasium.

Clerk: Well, how big is your gymnasium?

Sports Car

An old gent was passing a busy intersection when a large St. Bernard brushed against him and knocked him down. An instant later a foreign sports car skidded around the corner and inflicted more damage.

A bystander helped him up and asked him if the dog had hurt him. "Well," he answered, "the dog didn't hurt so much, but that tin can tied to his tail nearly killed me."

∽

Small car salesman to prospect: It only seats two but can easily accommodate fourteen bumper stickers.

Spring

Time of year when a young man's fancy turns to what the girls have been thinking about all winter.

Spurs

First cowboy: Why are you wearing only one spur?
Second cowboy: Well, I figure when one side of the horse starts running, the other side will too.

Squirrel

Wife: You don't expect me to wear this old squirrel coat the rest of my life do you?
Husband: Why not? The squirrels do!

Stalemate

A spouse who is beginning to smell musty.

Stationery Store

A store that stays pretty much at the same location.

Statistician

A liar who can figure.

Steak

Customer: Your sign says you will cook any type of steak. I'll try an elephant steak.
Waiter: Will that be African or Indian?

ᔌ

Waiter: And how did you find your steak, sir?
Customer: I just lifted one of the brussels sprouts and there it was!

Steel Wool

Ned: I am going to feed my sheep ironized yeast.
Jed: Why are you going to do that?
Ned: So I'll be able to get steel wool.

Stick 'Em Up

Coach (to referee): You stink!
Referee (who picked up the football, marked off another fifteen-yard penalty, and turned to the coach): How do I smell from here?

Stockbroker

A man who can take a bankroll and run it into a shoestring.

Stone

"My husband didn't leave a bit of insurance."
"Then where did you get that gorgeous diamond ring?"
"Well, he left $1,000 for his casket and $5,000 for a stone. This is the stone."

Stop the Presses

Newspaper misprint:
Lost: Gray and white male cat. Answers to electric can opener.

∽

Church bulletin misprint:
The church had a going-away party for Pastor Hanson. The congregation was anxious to give him a little momentum.

∽

Newspaper misprint:
Found: False teeth, in parking lot at the Walters Department Store. Please come in and smile at the switchboard operator, and she will return them to you.

∾

Church bulletin misprint:
Twenty-five year friendship ends at altar.

∾

Newspaper misprint:
Dead policeman on force 17 years.

∾

Newspaper misprint:
The Army has tested some new explosives recently. In fact, they dropped four-ton blondes on the test site.

∾

Newspaper misprint:
City officials talk rubbish.

∾

Misprinted sign:
Don't kill your wife. Let our washing machine do the dirty work.

∾

Church bulletin misprint:
Pastor Moore has spoken in the largest Baptist churches in America. To miss hearing him will be the chance of a lifetime!

∾

Newspaper misprint:
For Sale: Two plots in lively Fairmount Cemetery.

∞

Church bulletin misprint:
Ushers will swat latecomers at these points in the service.

∞

Newspaper misprint:
Clarksville, Tennessee, which calls itself the largest outdoor mule market in the world, held a mule parade yesterday, headed by the governor.

STRIFE

If you want to avoid domestic strife, don't marry in January . . . and that goes for the other months, too.

STRIKING SERMON

One which hits the man who is not there.

STUCCO

What you get when you sit on gummo.

STUPID

Are you naturally stupid or did a Cuban hijack your brain?

STUTTERER

A big hulk of a man, somewhat sinister in appearance, accosted a small, dapper gentleman on the street, and asked, "C-c-can you t-t-tell m-m-me how to g-g-get to C-C-City Hall?"

The small man paled and, turning on his heels fled down the street. Angered and exasperated, the big man pursued him. They raced for several blocks until the little man's wind gave out and he was overtaken and captured. The big man seized him by the arm and cried angrily, "W-w-what do you m-m-mean . . . running away w-w-when I ask y-y-you a c-c-civil question?"

The little man looked up and gasped, "D-d-do you t-t-think I w-w-wanted m-m-my block k-k-knocked off?"

SUCCESS

With some people success turns their heads. With others, too bad it doesn't wring their necks.

∽

The road to success is dotted with many tempting parking places.

∽

They say success is ninety percent perspiration—you must be a tremendous success!

SUED

Jack and Jill
Went up the hill
To fetch a pail
Of water.
Jack fell down
And broke his crown,
And sued the farmer
And his daughter.

SUGAR DADDY

One form of crystallized sap.

Suggestion Box

After examining the contents of the employees' suggestion box, the boss complained, "I wish they'd be more specific. What kind of kite? What lake?"

Sultan

Sultan to small boy: Go ask one of your mothers.

Sun

Did you hear about the fellow who stayed up all night wondering where the sun went? It finally dawned on him.

Sunbathe

My wife loves to sunbathe—she's a fry in the ointment.

Sunday

Q: What is the strongest day in the week?
A: Sunday. The rest are weekdays.

∽

Mother: You shouldn't be flying that model airplane in the backyard on Sunday.

Johnny: Oh, it is all right to fly this one. It isn't a pleasure plane. It's a missionary plane going to the jungle.

Sunday School

A Sunday school teacher asked a little girl, "What are the sins of omission?"

After some thought, she answered, "They're the sins we ought to have committed but haven't."

❧

Little Suzie: My Sunday school teacher says we're put on earth to help others. Is that right, Mom?
Mother: Of course, dear.
Little Suzie: Then what are the others here for?

❧

In a Sunday school class the teacher asked the students to write down the Ten Commandments. For the fifth commandment one boy put, "Humor thy father and thy mother."

❧

A Sunday school teacher asked her students to draw a picture of the Holy Family. After the pictures were brought to her, she saw that some of the youngsters had drawn the conventional pictures—the Holy Family and the manger, the Holy Family riding on the mule, etc.

But she called up one little boy to ask him to explain the drawing, which showed an airplane with four heads sticking out of the plane windows.

She said, "I can understand you drew three of the heads to show Joseph, Mary, and Jesus. But who's the fourth head?"

"Oh," answered the boy, "that's Pontius the pilot!"

❧

A little boy forgot his lines in a Sunday school presentation. His mother was in the front row to prompt him. She gestured and formed the words silently with her lips, but it did not help. Her son's memory was blank.

Finally she leaned forward and whispered the cue, "I am the light of the world."

The child beamed and with great feeling and a loud, clear voice said, "My mother is the light of the world."

❧

A young woman named Murphy was teaching a Sunday school class the 23rd Psalm. As the little voices chorused out, she seemed somewhere to detect a false note. She heard the children one by one, until at last she came across one little boy who was concluding the psalm with the words, "Surely good Miss Murphy shall follow me all the days of my life."

∽

Q: Do you know how you can tell that David was older than Goliath?
A: Because David rocked Goliath to sleep!

∽

A Sunday school teacher asked her class to write a composition on the story of Samson. One teenage girl wrote, "Samson wasn't so unusual. The boys I know brag about their strength and wear their hair long too."

∽

Sunday school teacher: How could Noah see in the dark?
Student: He had floodlighting on the ark.

∽

"Mommy," said little Judy, "did you ever see a cross-eyed bear?"
"Why, no, Judy," chuckled her mother. "But why do you ask?"
"Well, in Sunday school this morning, we sang about 'consecrated cross-eyed bear.'"

∽

Q: Who was the most popular actor in the Bible?
A: Samson. He brought the house down.

∽

Correcting Sunday school lessons one day, a teacher found that little Jimmy had written, "Harold be thy name," as well as "Give us this day our jelly bread."

∽

Fay: How long a period of time did Cain hate his brother?
Ray: As long as he was Abel.

SUPERIORITY

My kid sister has a superiority complex . . . she thinks she's almost as good as me.

SUPPER

Mother (to manager of a movie theater): Did my little boy come in here at 12:00? He had on a blue sweater and a red cap. He has blond hair.
Manager: Yes, he is sitting in the fourth row.
Mother: Do you mind giving him this package? It's his supper.

SURREY MAKERS

People who are always looking for fringe benefits.

SWAP

Seems that a tribal chieftain's daughter was offered as a bridge to the son of a neighboring potentate in exchange for two cows and four sheep. The big swap was to be effected on the shore of the steam that separated the two tribes. Pop and his daughter showed up at the appointed time only to discover that the groom and his livestock were on the other side of the stream. The father grunted, "The fool doesn't know which side his bride is bartered on."

SWEETHEART

Millionaire: What's your name, driver?
Driver: Alfred, sir.
Millionaire: I always call my drivers by their last names.
Driver: It's Sweetheart, sir.
Millionaire: Drive on, Alfred.

SWELLED-HEAD

Nature's frantic effort to fill a vacuum.

SWIMMING POOL

A crowd of people with water in it.

SYNTAX

A new tax that should bring in all the money the government needs.

❖ T ❖

TACT

What you think but don't say.

❧

Thinking all you say without saying all you think.

❧

The art of saying nothing when there is nothing to say.

TAILOR SHOP

Last of the big-time menders.

TAKING IT EASY

Nothing reminds a woman of all that needs to be done around the house like a husband who is taking it easy.

TALK

Trying to get a word in edgewise with some people is like trying to thread a sewing machine with the motor running.

❧

There's nothing wrong with having nothing to say—unless you insist on saying it.

❧

Fred: What's more clever than speaking several languages?
Sally: Keeping your mouth shut in one.

TALKING

Son: What do you call it when one is talking?
Dad: Monologue.
Son: What do you call it when two women are talking?
Dad: Cat-alogue.

∽

Young Tom told his father that when he grew up, he wanted to drive a big army tank.

"Well, son," said his dad, "if that's what you want to do, I certainly won't stand in your way."

TAP

Q: What is the best cure for water on the brain?
A: A tap on the head.

TARDY

In explaining her tardiness to English class, a high school junior stated demurely, "The boy who was following me walked very slowly."

TAXES

April 15 should be called Taxgiving day.

∽

Taxpayer: I always pay my income taxes all at once.
Tax collector: But you are allowed to pay them in quarterly installments.
Taxpayer: I know it, but my heart can't stand it four times a year.

∽

Joe: Did you know that some of the presidents gave their salaries back to the government?
Moe: That idea really caught on. Now they have us all doing it.

⌘

A man walked into the tax collector's office and sat down and smiled at everyone.
"May I help you?" said the clerk in charge.
"No," said the man. "I just wanted to meet the people I have been working for all these years."

⌘

Tax collector: Why don't you pay your taxes with a smile?
Taxpayer: I'd love to but you insist on money!

⌘

Conscience is that still small voice that tells you the Internal Revenue Service might check your return.

⌘

A distraught taxpayer handed in his income tax return with his check to the Internal Revenue agent.
"Boy," complained the man, "the boys in Washington are a heartless bunch. They sure cleaned out my bank account!"
"Cheer up," consoled the revenue man. "Remember what Benjamin Franklin said: 'Nothing is certain but death and taxes.'"
"Yeah," said the taxpayer. "I only wish they came in that order."

⌘

I'm a little worried about this year's income tax. I think I made it out wrong. I've got forty-two cents left.

⌘

I don't know if we'll ever get a cure for poverty, but the way taxes and prices are going up, we've got a sure cure for wealth!

∽

You should file your income tax, not chisel it.

Taxidermist

Man who knows his stuff.

Tea Bag

Kathy: My husband has dreadful table manners. He always holds his little pinky finger out when he holds a cup of tea.

Julie: In society it is considered polite to hold out your little pinky when drinking tea.

Kathy: With the tea bag hanging from it?

Teacher

Teacher: Johnny, give me a sentence with a direct object.
Johnny: Teacher, everybody thinks you're beautiful.
Teacher: Thank you, Johnny, but what is the object?
Johnny: A good report card.

∽

In the traffic court of a large midwestern city, a young lady was brought before the judge to answer a ticket given to her for driving through a red light. She explained to his honor that she was a school-teacher and requested an immediate disposal of her case in order that she might hasten on to her classes. A wild gleam came into the judge's eye. "You're a schoolteacher, eh?" said he. "Madam, I shall realize my lifelong ambition. I've waited years to have a schoolteacher in this court.

Sit down at that table and write 'I will not go through a red light' five hundred times!"

∽

Teacher: If I laid four eggs over there, and four eggs over here, how many eggs would I have?
Student: I don't think you can do it, teacher.

∽

He was in school so long the other pupils used to bring him apples thinking he was the teacher.

Teenager

A teenager is someone who can eat his heart out without affecting his appetite.

∽

Dialogue between teenager and parent:
"I'm off to the party."
"Well, have a good time."
"Look, Pop, don't tell me what to do."

∽

If you live in a house full of teenagers, it is not necessary to ask for whom the bell tolls. It's not for you.

∽

Dad: Did you use the car last night?
Son: Yes, Dad. I took some of the boys for a ride.
Dad: Well, tell them I found two of their lipsticks.

∽

About the time the bedtime stories are televised, many youngsters are going out for the evening.

∽

I know a teenage girl who had been trying to run away from home for a year but every time she gets to the front door the phone rings.

∽

Father: What's wrong, Judy? Usually you talk on the phone for hours. This time you only talked half an hour. How come?
Judy: It was the wrong number.

∽

Man to friend: By the time I found out my father was right, my son was old enough to disagree with me.

∽

Father of teenage son to neighbor: Junior's at that awkward age . . . too old for a spanking and too young for analysis.

∽

Son: Dad, the Bible says if you don't let me have the car, you hate me.
Father: Where does it say that?
Son: Proverbs 13:24—"He that spareth the rod hateth his son."

∽

Teenage daughter (as the radio ground out the final notes of the latest hit song): Did you ever hear anything so wonderful?
Father: Only once—when a truck loaded with empty milk cans bumped another truck filled with live ducks.

∽

Officer to man pacing sidewalk at 3 A.M.: What are you doing here?

Gentleman: I forgot my key, Officer, and I'm waiting for my children to come home and let me in.

Teenager: Mary was in tears the other night because she had nothing to wear for her date. All her sweatshirts were in the wash.

A message for all parents: Is your teenage son or daughter out for the evening? If so, take advantage of the opportunity. Pack your furniture, call a moving van, and don't leave a forwarding address.

Adolescence is a period of rapid changes. Between the ages of twelve and seventeen, for example, a child may see his parents age twenty years.

My boy is fifteen . . . going on twelve!

Adult education is what goes on in a household containing teenage children!

TELEPHONE

Mother: Is this telephone call really necessary?

Daughter: How can I tell before I've made it?

Did you hear about the teenager who plans to run away from home just as soon as she gets a long enough telephone extension cord?

Temperamental

Ninety percent temper; ten percent mental.

Tempt

"Keep your feet where they belong."
"Don't tempt me."

Ten Commandments

Husband: Wouldn't it be fun to go to the Holy Land and stand on Mount Sinai and shout out the Ten Commandments?
Wife: It would be better if you stayed home and kept them.

Tennis

A very overweight man was discussing his tennis game with a friend.
"My brain barks out commands to my body: Run forward speedily! Start right away! Hit the ball gracefully over the net! Get back into position!"
"Then what happens?" asked the friend.
"And then, my body says, 'Who, me?'"

Test

Student: I don't think I deserve a zero on this test!
Teacher: Neither do I, but it's the lowest mark I can give you.

Texan

A guide was showing a Texan Niagara Falls.
Guide: I'll bet you don't have anything like that in Texas.
Texan: Nope, I reckon we don't; but we got plumbers that could fix it.

☙

A Texas rancher was visiting an Iowa farm. The Iowa farmer was justly proud of this two hundred acres of rich, productive land.

"Is this your whole farm?" the Texan asked. "Why, back in Texas I get in my car at five o'clock in the morning, and I drive and drive all day. At dusk I just reach the end of my ranch."

The Iowa farmer thought a while and replied, "I used to have a car like that, too."

∽

The owner of a large ranch in Texas had fifty men working for him. None of them worked as hard as he expected them to work. One day he had an idea about how to cure his men of their laziness.

He called them together and said, "I've got a nice easy job for the laziest man on the ranch. Will the laziest man please step forward." Every man stepped forward except one man.

"Why don't you step over with the rest of the men?" asked the rancher.

"Too much trouble," said the man.

THEOLOGY

Division has done more to hide Christ from the view of all men than all the infidelity that has ever been spoken.

THIEF

A person who has the habit of finding things before the owner loses them.

THINK

The person who thinks before he speaks is silent most of the time.

∽

My wife and I always think exactly alike, only she usually has the first think.

Thor

The thunder god went for a ride
Upon his favorite filly.
"I'm Thor," he cried.
The horse replied,
"You forgot your thaddle, thilly."

Thought

The main reason that some of us get lost in thought is that it is such unfamiliar territory.

Three-Headed Monster

A little boy came home from school crying, "Mommy, Mommy. The kids at school called me a three-headed monster."
The mother responded sympathetically: "Now, there, there, there."

Thumb

A modern means of transportation.

Tibet

A housewife in Tibet smelled something burning in the kitchen, rushed in, and saw smoke pouring out of the oven. "Oh, my baking yak!" she said.

Tiger

He who rides a tiger is afraid to dismount.

TIME

The shortest known unit is the time between the change of the traffic light and the honk from the kook behind you.

∽

Pilot: Control tower, what time is it?
Control tower: What airline is this?
Pilot: What difference does that make?
Control tower: If it is United Airlines, it is 6:00 P.M.; if it is TWA, it is 1800 hours; if it is Ozark, the big hand is on the. . . .

TIRED

"I think I labor too hard sometimes. I'm a farmer and I work fifteen hours a day, seven days a week."
"What do you grow?"
"Very tired."

TITANIC

Q: What do you get if you cross the Atlantic on the *Titanic*?
A: Very wet.

TITLE

In an age when everyone seems to be playing the name game of glorifying job titles, the man in charge of the meat department at a store in Wichita Falls, Texas, deserves a round of applause. On his weekly time card he describes his position as "Meat Head."

TOM

"My name is T-t-t-t-tom."
"I'll call you Tom for short."

Tongue

A loose tongue often gets its owner into a tight place.

∽

When you are in deep water, it's a good idea to keep your mouth shut.

∽

Once when C.H. Spurgeon, then a young man, was passing by the house of a woman with a poison tongue, she let him have a volley of impolite words. "Yes, thank you; I am quite well," Spurgeon said. Then she let out another volley. "Yes, it does look as if it's going to rain," he replied.

Surprised, the woman exclaimed, "Bless the man, he's deaf as a post! What's the use of talking to him?"

∽

An old philosopher of Greece once received a severe tongue-lashing from his wife. When he listened in silence, she was more infuriated; so she picked up a pail of cold water and threw it over him, drenching him from head to foot.

With the water still dripping from him, very calmly he remarked, "After that thunder and lightning, I rather expected a shower."

Tongue Sandwich

"I seem to be a rose between two thorns," remarked Miss Prettygirl as she seated herself between two men at a football game.

"I'd say it's more like a tongue sandwich," retorted one of the men.

Tongue Twisters

Six gray geese on green grass grazing.

∽

Copper coffee pot.

❧

Ziggy Jazinski.

❧

Bill had a billboard. Bill also had a board bill. The board bill bored Bill, so Bill sold the billboard to pay his board bill. So after Bill sold his billboard to pay his board bill, the board bill no longer bored Bill.

❧

If a Hottentot tutor taught a Hottentot tot
To talk 'ere the tot could totter,
Ought the Hottentot be taught to say aught?
Or, what ought to be taught her?
If to hoot and toot a Hottentot tot
Be taught by a Hottentot tutor,
Should the tutor get hot if the Hottentot tot
Hoots and toots at the Hottentot tutor?

TOOTHPASTE

Did you hear about the new toothpaste that has shoe polish in it? It is for people who put their feet in their mouths.

❧

Did you hear about the new toothpaste with food particles in it? It is for people who can't eat before brushing.

TOTAL

The sum total of our national debt is some total.

TOURIST

A person who travels one thousand miles to get a picture of himself standing by his car.

TOWER OF BABEL

Q: What was the Tower of Babel?
A: Wasn't that where Solomon kept his wives?

TOWN

Native: What do you think of our little town?
Traveler: It's the first cemetery I've ever seen with traffic lights.

TRAFFIC COURT

Sign at a traffic court: Don't Complain, Think Of The Summonses You Have Deserved But Didn't Get!

TRAFFIC LIGHT

A little green light that changes to red as your car approaches.

TRAIN

At a commuter train station a policeman noticed a woman driver bowed over the steering wheel of her car.

"Is there anything wrong?" said the policeman.

Half crying and half laughing the woman responded, "For ten years I have driven my husband to the station to catch his train. This morning I forgot him!"

∽

Two men were riding on a train for the first time. They brought bananas for lunch. Just as one of them bit into his banana, the train entered a tunnel.

First man: Did you take a bite of your banana?

Second man: No.

First man: Well, don't. I did and went blind!

Train to Buffalo

A big executive boarded a New York to Chicago train. He explained to the porter: "I'm a heavy sleeper and I want you to be sure to wake me at 3:00 A.M. to get off in Buffalo. Regardless of what I say, get me up, for I have some important business there."

The next morning he awakened in Chicago. He found the porter and really poured it on with abusive language.

After he had left, someone said, "How could you stand there and take that kind of talk from that man?"

The porter said, "That ain't nothing. You should have heard what the man said that I put off in Buffalo."

Trapeze Artist

A guy who gets the hang of things.

Tree

Something that will stand in the same place for sixty years and then suddenly jump in front of a car.

Triumph

Triumph is just "umph" added to "try."

Trojan Horse

A phony pony.

TROUBLES

So you think you have troubles! When I got to the building, I found that the hurricane had knocked some bricks off the top. So I rigged up a beam with a pulley at the top of the building and hoisted up a couple of barrels full of bricks. When I had fixed the building, there were a lot of bricks left over. Then I went to the bottom of the building and cast off the line. Unfortunately, the barrel of bricks was heavier than I was, and before I knew what was happening, the barrel started down, jerking me off the ground.

I decided to hang on and halfway up I met the barrel coming down and received a hard blow on the shoulder. I then continued to the top, banging my head against the beam and getting my fingers jammed in the pulley. When the barrel hit the ground it burst its bottom, allowing all the bricks to spill out.

I was now heavier than the barrel and so started down again at high speed. Halfway down I met the barrel coming up and received more injuries to my shins.

When I hit the ground, I landed on the bricks, getting several painful cuts. At this point I must have lost my presence of mind because I let go of the line. The barrel came down, giving me another heavy blow on the head and putting me in the hospital.

I respectfully requested sick leave.

☙

Remember this before you burden other people with your troubles. Half of them aren't the least bit interested, and the rest are delighted that you're getting what they think is coming to you.

TRUTH

Wife to husband: I don't mind your little half-truths, but you keep telling me the wrong half.

☙

Pompous politician: I was never whipped but once in my life, and that was for telling the truth.
Heckler: It sure cured you, didn't it?

TRYING

Mother: Johnny, this isn't a very good report card. Are you trying?
Johnny: Yes, my teacher said I am the most trying boy in the class.

∽

Mother, having finally tucked a small boy into bed after an unusually trying day: Well, I've worked today from son-up to son-down!

TURKEY

"I'd let those doctors experiment on me for the sake of science. I'm not afraid. I've gone through the war. Why, once I even volunteered to let them put a new heart into my chest if one was available that suited my character."
"What was the matter? Couldn't they find a chicken big enough?"

TURN SIGN

A lady made a right-hand turn from the left-hand lane and promptly collided with another car. The driver got out and accosted her.
"Lady, why didn't you signal?"
"Mister, I always turn here."

TURTLE

A reptile who lives in a mobile home.

TWIN BELLIES

He has T.B.—Twin Bellies.

TWINS

Melba: I guess your husband was pleased when he found himself the father of twin boys.

Pam: Was he! He went around grinning from heir to heir.

∽

Jill: Are you an only child?
Bill: No, used to be twins.
Jill: When were you twins?
Bill: My father has a picture of me when I was two.

TYPING

"Miss Hatfield, I was just reading over this letter you did. Your typing is really improving. I see there are only seven mistakes here."

"Thank you, sir."

"Now, let's take a look at the second line."

❧ U ❧

UGLY

A man sent his picture to the Lonely Hearts Club. The reply came back, "We're not that lonely."

❧

Paul: I once had a beard like yours, and when I saw how terrible I looked, I immediately cut it off.

Saul: I used to have a face like yours, too. And when I saw how terrible it made me look, I immediately grew a beard.

❧

She has early-American features . . . she looks like a buffalo.

❧

Man (to woman on train): That is the ugliest baby I have ever seen!

Woman: Conductor! Conductor! This man has just insulted my baby!

Conductor: Now, Madam, don't get mad. I'll get a drink of water for you and a banana for your baby.

❧

Auntie: When I was a child, I was told if I made ugly faces I would stay like it.

Little Joan: Well, you can't say you weren't warned, Auntie.

❧

"You look pretty dirty, Susie."

"Thank you. I look pretty when I'm clean, too."

❧

I don't recall your face, but your breath is familiar!

∽

Is that your head, or did your body blow a bubble?

∽

Is that your face, or did your neck throw up?

Umbrella

The man of the house finally took all the disabled umbrellas to the repairer's. Two days later, on his way to his office, he got up to leave the streetcar and absentmindedly laid hold of the umbrella belonging to a woman beside him. The woman cried, "Stop, thief!" rescued her umbrella and covered the man with shame and confusion.

The same day, he stopped at the repairer's and received all eight of his umbrellas duly repaired. As he entered a streetcar, with the unwrapped umbrellas tucked under his arm, he was horrified to behold glaring at him the lady of his morning adventure. Her voice came to him charged with withering scorn: "Huh! Had a good day, didn't you!"

Unabated

A mousetrap without any cheese or a fishhook without a worm.

Unabridged

A river you have to wade across.

Uncle Sam

The one who wears a tall hat so he can pass it around.

UNDERTAKER

"Do you believe in the survival of the fittest?"
"I don't believe in the survival of anybody. I am the undertaker."

∽

"I just found out your uncle's an undertaker. I thought you told me he was a doctor."
"Nope, I just said he followed the medical profession."

UNISON

An only male child.

UNITED STATES

A Russian was about to be sentenced to Siberia and said to his captors, "If the United States is such a terrible place, why not send me there instead?"

UNLUCKY

Kenny: I think we had better get going Friday.
Lenny: Not Friday. That's an unlucky day.
Kenny: I was born on Friday, and I don't think it's unlucky.
Lenny: Yeah, but what do your parents think?

UNTOLD WEALTH

That which does not appear on the income tax returns.

Vacation

Jack: You didn't take a vacation this year, did you?
Mack: No, I thought I needed a rest.

∽

"Remember on our vacation when we spent money like there was no tomorrow? Well, it's tomorrow."

∽

The smog was so bad in Los Angeles that I felt the sights and went back home!

∽

A traveling salesman was held up in the West by a storm and flood. He wired his office in New York: DELAYED BY STORM. SEND INSTRUCTIONS.
His boss wired back: COMMENCE VACATION IMMEDIATELY.

∽

If you can't get away for a vacation, just tip every third person you meet and you'll get the same effect.

Valuable Sense of Humor

One that enables a person to see instantly what isn't safe to laugh at.

Vanguard

A person who protects trucks.

VASE

Benjie: Mom, do you remember that vase you always worried I would break?
Mom: Yes, what about it?
Benjie: Your worries are over.

VENETIAN BLIND

Sign on car of a venetian-blind salesman: Watch Out! Blind Man Driving!

VENTRILOQUIST

A person who talks to himself for a living.

VERBOSITY

Inebriated with the exuberance of his own verbosity.
—*Benjamin Disraeli*

VICE PRESIDENT

A man who had just been promoted to vice president boasted of it so much to his wife that she finally said, "Vice presidents are a dime a dozen. Why, in the supermarket they even have a vice president of prunes!"

Furious, the husband phoned the supermarket with the expectation of refuting his wife. He asked to speak to the vice president in charge of prunes.

"Which one?" was the reply. "Packaged or bulk prunes?"

VICIOUS CIRCLE

Bad company.

Voice

Pretty young student: Professor Boschovich, do you think I will ever be able to do anything with my voice?

Weary teacher: Well, it might come in handy in case of fire or shipwreck.

WAITER, OH WAITER!

Customer: Waiter! I can't seem to find any oysters in this oyster soup.
Waiter: Would you expect to find angels in angel food cake?

❧

Customer: Waiter! I'm so hungry I could eat a horse!
Waiter: You certainly came to the right place.

❧

Customer: Waiter! I'll have some kidleys.
Waiter: Do you mean kidneys, sir?
Customer: That's what I said, didle I?

❧

Customer: Waiter! This sausage has meat at one end and bread at the other.
Waiter: Well, sir, you know how hard it is to make both ends meet these days.

❧

Customer: No, I won't have any mushrooms, waiter. I was nearly poisoned by them last week.
Waiter: Is that so? Then I've won my bet with the cook!

❧

Customer: Waiter! This food is terrible. I won't eat it! You had better get the manager.
Waiter: Won't do any good, mister. The manager wouldn't eat it either.

❧

Waiter: Would you like your coffee black?
Customer: What other colors do you have?

∽

Customer: Is your water supply healthy?
Waiter: Yes, sir. We only use well water.

∽

Customer: Waiter! There's no chicken in my chicken soup!
Waiter: There's no horse in the horseradish either.

∽

Waiter: How's the soup, sir?
Diner: To tell you the truth, I'm really sorry I stirred it.

∽

Tim: Look, Jim, why are you always trying to impress me? So you spoke to the waiter in French! So, big deal! So what good is it to know French? . . . What did he tell you, waiter?
Waiter: He told me to give you the check, sir!

∽

Waiter: We haven't had a complaint in twenty-five years.
Customer: No wonder. The customers all starve to death before they are served.

∽

Customer: Waiter, will you bring me another sandwich, please?
Waiter: Will there be anything else?
Customer: Yes, a paperweight. My first sandwich blew away.

∽

The lady said to the waitress, "May I have a bag to carry leftovers to my dog?"

Her six-year old said: "Oh Mother, are we going to get a dog?"

∽

Customer: What flavors of ice cream do you have?

Hoarse waitress: Vanilla, strawberry, and chocolate.

Customer: Do you have laryngitis?

Waitress: No; just vanilla, strawberry, and chocolate.

∽

Customer: Do you serve crabs in this dump?

Waiter: Yes, sir; what'll you have?

∽

Percy: I won't criticize their chef, but you'll notice three shakers on every table . . . salt, pepper, and Alka-Seltzer.

∽

"Waiter!" shouted an irate customer. "I can't tell whether this is coffee or tea! It tastes like benzine!"

"If it tastes like benzine then it positively is coffee," the waiter said. "Our tea tastes like turpentine."

∽

"Waiter," said the surprised customer as he examined his check, "what's this eight dollars for?"

"For the chopped liver sandwich, sir."

"Yeah?" The customer nodded. "Whose liver was it? Rockefeller's?"

∽

Someday I would like to see a waiter with enough courage to lay the check face-up on the table.

∽

A man walked into a restaurant in a strange town. The waiter came and asked him for his order. Feeling lonely, he replied, "Meat loaf and a kind word." When the waiter returned with the meat loaf, the man said, "Where's the good word?" The waiter put down the meat loaf and sighed, bent down and whispered, "Don't eat the meat loaf."

The manager of a restaurant called his waitresses together. "Girls," he began, "I want you all to look your best today. Greet every customer with a smile, put on a little extra makeup, and see to it that your hair is in place."

"What's up?" asked one of the girls. "Bunch of big shots coming in today?"

"No, the meat's tough today."

Customer: Waiter! There's a fly in my soup!
Waiter: It can't be, sir. You're eating a noon lunch . . . and this is a fly-by-night place.

Diner: What would you recommend for tonight?
Waiter: Go someplace else . . . the cook is on strike.

WALKIE-TALKIE

The opposite of sittie-sittie.

WALL STREET

"I hear that your uncle lost his wealth on Wall Street."

"Yes, that is true. He was standing on the corner and dropped his last quarter into the sewer."

WARGAMES

An Army base staff that was planning war games did not want to use live ammunition. Instead they informed the men: "In place of a rifle, you go, 'Bang, bang.' In place of a knife, you go, 'Stab, stab.' In place of a hand grenade, you go, 'Lob, lob.'"

The game was in progress when one of the soldiers saw one of the enemy. He went, "Bang, bang," but nothing happened. He ran forward and went, "Stab, stab," but nothing happened. He ran back and went, "Lob, lob," but nothing happened. Finally he walked up to the enemy and said, "You are not playing fair. I went, 'Bang, bang,' and 'Stab, stab,' and 'Lob, lob,' and you haven't fallen dead yet!"

The enemy responded, "Rumble, rumble. I'm a tank."

WART

Willy: They tell me that the way to get rid of a wart is to bury a cat. Do you think that will work?

Billy: Yes, if the wart is on the cat.

～

A man walked into a doctor's office with a frog growing out of his ear.

Doctor: When did you first notice it?

Frog: It started with a wart.

WASHINGTON

Washington, D.C.: Fund city.

WEAKNESS

Don't judge your wife too harshly for her weaknesses. If she didn't have them, chances are she would never have married you.

WEATHER

Probably the last completely accurate weather forecast was when God told Noah there was a one hundred percent chance of precipitation.

☙

Postcard to Weather Bureau: "Sirs: I thought you would be interested in knowing that I have just shoveled three feet of partly cloudy from my front steps."

WEATHER GAUGE

A tourist stopped at a country gas station. While his car was being serviced, he noticed an old-timer basking in the sun with a piece of rope in his hand. The tourist walked up to the old-timer and asked, "What do you have there?"

"That's a weather gauge, sonny," the old-timer replied.

"How can you possibly tell the weather with a piece of rope?"

"It's simple," said the old-timer. "When it swings back and forth, it's windy. And when it gets wet, it's raining."

WEDDING

Christy: Do you think it's unlucky to postpone a wedding?
Lisa: Not if you keep on doing it.

☙

"It's a dollar and sense wedding."
"What do you mean?"
"He hasn't a dollar and she hasn't any sense."

WEIGHT

Wife: I've lost quite a lot of weight.
Husband: I don't see it.
Wife: Sure you don't. I've lost it.

☙

WELL-DRESSED

General Custer was a well-dressed man. When they found him he was wearing an Arrow shirt.

WELL-INFORMED

You can always tell when a man's well-informed. His views are pretty much like your own.

WHAT'S FUNNY?

Two men went to the train station with a friend. The train was late so they sat down for a cup of coffee. They talked and drank and forgot about the train. Suddenly they heard the last announcement about the departing train. They all got up and started running. They ran down the tracks as the train was pulling out of the station. Two of the men made it to the last car and the third man was just not fast enough. The third man slowed to a stop and started laughing. An onlooker went up to the laughing man and said, "What are you laughing for? You just missed your train."

"You're right," was the reply. "I did miss my train. What's funny is those two men came to see me off."

WHISKERS

"He spilled rum on his whiskers and when lighting his cigarette his whiskers caught on fire."

"What did he do then?"

"Oh, he just fiddled with his whiskers while rum burned."

∽

Q: Why are there so few men with whiskers in heaven?
A: Because most men get in by a close shave.

WHITEHOUSE

Honorable mansion.

WHO PAYS THE BILL?

In reply to your request to send a check, I wish to inform you that the present condition of my bank account makes it almost impossible.

My shattered financial conditions are due to federal laws, corporation laws, mother-in-law, brother-in-law, sisters-in-law, and outlaws.

Through these taxes I am compelled to pay a business tax, assessment tax, head tax, school tax, income tax, casket tax, food tax, furniture tax, sales tax, and excise tax. Even my brain is taxed.

I am required to get a business license, car license, hunting license, fishing license, truck and auto license, not to mention marriage and dog license. I am also required to contribute to every society and organization which the genius of man is capable of bringing into life; to women's relief, unemployed relief, and gold digger's relief. Also to every hospital and charitable institution in the city, including the Red Cross, the Black Cross, the Purple Cross, and the Double Cross.

For my own safety, I am compelled to carry life insurance, liability insurance, burglary insurance, accident insurance, property insurance, business insurance, earthquake insurance, tornado insurance, unemployment insurance, old age insurance, and fire insurance.

My own business is so governed that it is no easy matter for me to find out who owns it. I am inspected, suspected, disrespected, rejected, dejected, and compelled until I provide an inexhaustible supply of money for every known need of the human race.

Simply because I refuse to donate something or another I am boycotted, talked about, lied about, held up, held down, and robbed until I am almost ruined. I can tell you honestly that except for a miracle that happened I could not enclose this check. The wolf that comes to my door nowadays just had pups in my kitchen. I sold them and here's the money.

Would like more business to pay more taxes.

Sincerely yours,

WIFE

If your wife wants to learn to drive, don't stand in her way.

My wife is such a bad driver—she got three tickets on her written test.

❧

A husband was reading a newspaper when he came across the following advertisement:

"What we want is a night watchman who will be alert and ready for the slightest noise or indication of a burglar. Somebody who can sleep with one eye and both ears open and is not afraid to tackle anything."

Husband: Honey, I think I found the job you are looking for.

WILL

Lawyer: What's so different about your will?

Man: I want to leave everything to my wife only if she marries again. I want to be sure someone is sorry when I'm gone.

❧

"My uncle changed his will six times in three years."

"Aha! A fresh heir fiend!"

❧

Do you want to know a way to drive people crazy? Walk up to a complete stranger and say, "It's good to see you again, you lucky dog. So you finally struck it rich! Well, see you at the reading of the will."

Then rush away before that person can say anything.

WINDJAMMER

A person who spreads jelly on bread during a hurricane.

WINDOW

"Did you hear the story about the window you couldn't see through?"

"No."

"Well, that's okay . . . it's too dirty to tell anyway!"

Wisdom

The older I grow the more I distrust the familiar doctrine that age brings wisdom.

∽

He that gets money before he gets wit,
Will be but a short while master of it.

∽

It is wit to pick a lock and steal a horse, but wisdom to let them alone.

Wish

Husband: Why do you always wish for something you haven't got?
Wife: What else could one wish for?

Wit

Use your wit as a buckler, not as a sword.

∽

Wit is a good servant, but a bad master.
                                    —*Talleyrand*

∽

The wittiest man laughs least.

∽

A fool attempting to be witty
Is an object of profoundest pity.

WITS

Bill: I have had to make a living by my wits.
Gill: Well, half a living is better than none.

WIVES

Men do not know their wives well; but wives know their husbands perfectly.

WOLF

A girl can be scared to death by a mouse or a spider, but she's often too willing to take her chances with a wolf.

∽

A sailor has been called a wolf in ship's clothing.

WOMAN

On one issue, at least, men and women agree; they both distrust women.

∽

Woman begins resisting man's advances and ends by blocking his retreat.

∽

A good woman inspires a man, a brilliant woman interests him, a beautiful woman fascinates him—but a sympathetic woman gets him.

∽

A woman without religion is as a flower without scent.

∽

The reason women live longer than men is because paint is a great preservative.

∽

Women like the simpler things of life—men.

WOMEN'S LIB

Did you hear about Glena Zimmerman? She got involved in the women's lib movement and changed her name to Glena Zimmerperson.

∽

A women's lib speaker was addressing a large group and said, "Where would man be today if it were not for woman?"
She paused a moment and looked around the room.
"I repeat, where would man be today if it were not for woman?"
From the back of the room came a voice, "He'd be in the Garden of Eden eating strawberries."

∽

A girl involved with the women's lib movement boarded a crowded bus and one man rose to his feet.
"No, you must not give up your seat. I insist," she said.
"You may insist as much as you like, lady," was the reply. "This is the street where I get off."

WORK

The only man who ever got all his work done by Friday was Robinson Crusoe.

∽

If lawyers are disbarred and ministers unfrocked, perhaps electricians get delighted . . . Far Eastern diplomats disoriented . . . cashiers distilled . . . alpine climbers dismounted . . . piano tuners unstrung . . . orchestra leaders disbanded . . . artists' models deposed . . . cooks deranged . . . nudists redressed . . . office clerks defiled . . . mediums dispirited . . . dressmakers unbiased.

∽

Work—an unpopular way of earning money.

∽

The following announcement was placed on the bulletin board of a large company.

To all employees: Because of increased competition and a keen desire to remain in business, we find it necessary to institute a new policy. Effective immediately, we are asking that somewhere between starting and quitting time—without infringing too much on the time devoted to lunch period, coffee breaks, rest periods, storytelling, ticket-selling, golfing, auto racing, vacation planning, and rehashing of yesterday's TV programs—that each employee try to find some time that can be set aside to be known as The Work Break.

∽

First man: Why do you wear dark glasses?
Second man: Because I can't bear to see my wife work so hard.

∽

One day Johnny's father brought his boss home for dinner. When Johnny's mother served the meat, the little boy asked, "Is this mutton?" His mother replied, "No. Why do you ask?" "Because Dad said he was going to bring home a muttonhead for dinner," Johnny answered.

∽

Applicant: Before I take this job, tell me: Are the hours long?
Employer: No, only sixty minutes each.

∽

"So your sister got fired?"

"Yes. But she was going to leave anyway. Her boss is so conceited—he thinks the words can only be spelled his way."

∽

One employee to another employee: When the boss' son starts working here tomorrow, he'll have no special privileges or authority. Treat him just as you would anyone else who was due to take over the whole business in a year or two.

∽

"My brother's got a job in an electric shop. One day he grabbed hold of a live wire."

"What happened?"

"I don't know—but it's the only job he ever held on to."

∽

The only time people work like a horse is when the boss rides them.

∽

When some people retire, nobody knows the difference.

∽

A third grader went home and told her mother she was in love with a classmate and was going to marry him. "That's fine," said her mother, going along with the gag. "Does he have a job?"

The little girl replied, "Oh, yes. He erases the blackboard in our class."

∽

Nothing is as embarrassing as watching your boss do something you assured him couldn't be done.

∽

Husband (reading the morning paper): Another cup of coffee!
Wife: Aren't you going to the office today?
Husband: Oh, my goodness. I thought I was at the office!

∽

Nobody is sicker than the man who is sick on his day off.

∽

Son: Dad, this magazine article says that my birthstone is the ruby. What is yours?
Father: The grindstone.

∽

Boss: What's the idea of coming in here late every morning?
Employee: It's your fault. You have trained me so thoroughly not to watch the clock in the office, now I'm in the habit of not looking at it at home.

∽

Two men were digging a ditch on a very hot day. One said to the other, "Why are we down in this hole digging a ditch when our boss is standing up there under the shade of a tree?"

"I don't know," responded the other. "I'll ask him." So he climbed out of the hole and went to his boss. "Why are we digging in the hot sun and you are standing in the shade?"

"Intelligence," the boss said.

"What do you mean, 'intelligence'?"

The boss said, "Well, I'll show you. I'll put my hand on this tree and I want you to hit it with your fist as hard as you can." The ditch-digger took a mighty swing and tried to hit the boss' hand. The boss removed his hand and the ditchdigger hit the tree. The boss said, "That's intelligence!"

The ditchdigger went back to his hole. His friend asked, "What did he say?"

"He said we are down here because of intelligence."

"What's intelligence?" said the friend.

The ditchdigger put his hand on his face and said, "Take your shovel and hit my hand."

∽

Employer: We can pay you eighty dollars a week now and one hundred dollars a week in eight months.

Applicant: Thank you. I'll drop back in eight months.

∽

I just found out why I feel tired all the time: We made a survey and found I was doing more than my share of the world's work.

The population of the country is 160 million, but there are 62 million people over 60 years of age. That leaves 98 million to do the work. People under 21 years of age total 54 million, which leaves 44 million to do the work.

Then there are 21 million who are employed by the government, and that leaves 23 million to do the work. Ten million are in the Armed Forces—that leaves 13 million to do the work. Now deduct 12,800,000—the number in state and city offices—and that leaves 200,000 to do the work. There are 126,000 in hospitals, insane asylums, and so forth—that leaves 74,000 people to do the work.

But 62,000 of these refuse to work, so that leaves 12,000 to do the work. Now it may interest you to know that there are 11,988 people in jail, so that leaves just *two* people to do all the work and that's *you* and *me* and I'm getting tired doing everything myself.

∽

"Do you believe in life after death?" the boss asked one of his younger employees.

"Yes, sir."

"Well, then, that makes everything just fine," the boss went on. "About an hour after you left yesterday to go to your grandfather's funeral, he stopped in to see you."

∽

Boss: The main thing to remember is that repetition, repetition, repetition is the keynote! If you have a product to sell, keep harping on it every possible way, cram it down people's throats . . . make yourself sickening and repulsive if you have to, but don't ever forget to repeat and repeat and repeat! It's the only way to get results!

Employee: Yes, sir.

Boss: And now, what was it you came in to see me about?

Employee: Well, sir, a raise! A raise! A raise! A raise! A raise! A raise! A raise! A raise! . . .

WORRY

"You sure look worried."

"Man, I've got so many troubles that if anything happens to me today, it'll be at least two weeks before I can worry about it."

∽

Red: I'd give a thousand dollars to anyone who would do my worrying for me.

Ted: You're on. Where's the thousand?

Red: That's your first worry.

∽

Three out of four things you worry about happening don't happen; and three out of four things you don't worry about happening, do. Which all goes to prove that even if you're worrying about the wrong things, you're doing just about the right amount of worrying!

WORSE

I took her for better or worse—but she's much worse than I took her for.

WORTH

It's not what you pay a man, but what he costs you that counts.

—*Will Rogers*

Wrecked

Pretty young girl to friend: Not only has Jack broken my heart and wrecked my whole life, but he has spoiled my entire evening!

Wrinkle

Show me a wrinkle, and I'll show you the nick of time.

Writer

Writer: I dream up my stories.
Editor: You must dread going to bed.

✎

Writer: Can't you suggest something to put a finishing touch on my story?
Editor: Yes. A match.

✎

A tiger was walking through the jungle one day and saw two men relaxing under a tree. One was reading a newspaper, and the other was working feverishly on a manual typewriter.

The tiger leapt on the man with the newspaper, and ate him up. The tiger did not bother the other man at all. That's because any predator knows that readers digest but writers cramp.

Wrong Way

A policeman stopped a man driving the wrong way on a one-way street. "Didn't you see the arrow?" he demanded.

"Arrow? Honest, officer, I didn't even see the Indians."

❖ Y ❖

You Sure Told Them

There was a certain energetic young preacher who had a thriving country church. He was always prodding his people to do greater things for God. He spent much time in preparation of his sermons. There was a deacon in his congregation who did little and seemed to care less. It caused the young preacher much concern. On several occasions, the preacher would tell him exactly what he thought. The old deacon never caught the point. The old deacon always thought he was referring to someone else. One Sunday, the preacher made it plainer as to whom he was talking. Following the service the deacon said, "Preacher, you sure told them today."

The next sermon was still more pointed than ever. Again the deacon said, "Preacher, you sure told them today."

The next Sunday it rained so hard that no one was at the church except this one deacon. The preacher thought that he would now know about whom he was talking. The sermon went straight to the deacon who was the only one in the congregation. Following the service, the deacon walked up to the preacher and said, "Preacher, you sure told them if they had been here."

❧ Z ❧

Zoo

A family of lions feeding in the African Safari Park looked up as a car crammed with eight tourists pulled close to them.

"It's cruel," said the papa lion to his family, "to keep them caged up like that!"

∾

Q: Do you know what happened to the pregnant lady who got frightened by the bear at the zoo?

A: Her baby was born with bare feet!